So powerf
tions only
tions bef(
respectab.
great deal of fun resea.
also learned to question and chec.
thing I read. I would advise you to do the
same with everything you read – including
this book.

By the same author

Things You Didn't Know, You Didn't Know!

THINGS YOU THOUGHT YOU THOUGHT YOU KNEW!

GRAEME DONALD

London
UNWIN PAPERBACKS
Boston   Sydney

First published in Great Britain by Unwin Paperbacks 1986
This book is copyright under the Berne Convention. No reproduction
without permission. All rights reserved.

UNWIN ® PAPERBACKS
40 Museum Street, London WC1A 1LU, UK

Unwin Paperbacks
Park Lane, Hemel Hempstead, Herts HP2 4TE, UK

Allen & Unwin Australia Pty Ltd
8 Napier Street, North Sydney, NSW 2060, Australia

Unwin Paperbacks with the
Port Nicholson Press
PO Box 11–838 Wellington, New Zealand

© Graeme Donald 1986

British Library Cataloguing in Publication Data

Donald, Graeme
    Things you thought you thought you knew.
1. Curiosities and wonders
I. Title
032'.02   AG243
ISBN 0-04-827159-4

Set in 10 on 11½ point Sabon by Columns, Reading, Berkshire
and printed in Great Britain by
Cox and Wyman Ltd, Reading

For my mother, Norma, without whom this book would have been wholly impossible — and that's no misconception.

A

ABORIGINE

Although many would argue the point vigorously, *aborigine* does not, by definition, refer to the native population of Australia in particular. The first people to be so called were the Latin tribes of ancient Central Italy, and of Latin derivation itself, the word simply means 'from the beginning'. The OED makes no mention of Australia at all in its definition of the word but simply states that it describes people, animals or plant life indigenous to an area. So, the Australian native is an aborigine, but an aborigine is not necessarily an Australian native. One could equally describe Scots native to Scotland as aborigines, although such a foolhardy exercise in semantics would be unwise in the extreme in a Glasgow pub at closing time.

ACUTENESS OF HEARING IS INCREASED IN BLIND PEOPLE

The misfortune of being born blind or suddenly finding oneself in that situation is not compensated for by any increase in aural efficiency. What does happen is that blind people learn to use their hearing with more discrimination than sighted people, the increase in efficiency being more mental than physical. Their interpretation of sounds about them is more accurate, but it is not true that they will be able to pick up sounds indiscernible to the average sighted person unless they happen to be blessed with above average hearing in the first place. The myth has been reinforced over the years by the fact that a high proportion of piano-tuners seemed to be blind, but such choice of trade was made for the practical reason that the location and order of the tuning pegs are universally the same, so only a limited degree of 'manual' search is required. Only those blind people who had a sufficiently musical ear anyway followed this trade, others became telephone operators or audio typists for exactly the same reasons.

ADAM AND EVE AND THE GARDEN OF EDEN

Presuming that you accept the Bible's version of the so-called Creation, there are several misconceptions attached to these two characters which have been perpetuated down the ages by artists and clergy alike.

First, let's look at the 'apple'. Genesis 3 simply refers to 'the fruit' and never gets more specific. That it was an apple is less than likely since Mesopotamia, where the Garden of Eden is traditionally held to have been, is far too hot for apple cultivation. The apricot is a good contender but the most likely culprit as the fruit of the Tree of Knowledge is the fig, since it is only after having a nibble that Adam and Eve start rowing and sporting fig leaves to bury their differences. It was Aquila of Pontus who first started talking about apples when he translated the Song of Solomon from Hebrew into Greek. His choice of fruit was dictated by the fact that in his culture the apple symbolised desire and even lust. No one, and that includes St Jerome who translated the Old Testament into Latin, ever checked up, and the myth lived happily ever after.

Finally, there is the belief that God gave Adam and Eve their marching orders out of anger at their having disobeyed his instructions to leave the Tree of Knowledge strictly alone. Actually, he drove them out 'lest he put forth his hand, and take also of the Tree of Life, and eat, and live for ever'. So it was divine concern at the prospect of man achieving immortality that prompted the eviction.

'AIN'T' AIN'T GOOD ENGLISH

The word may well get sneered at in so-called polite company, but only if such company is wholly ignorant of that which constitutes perfectly acceptable English. The term is nothing more than a shortened form of 'am not' and can be written as 'an't', or as the more familiar 'ain't'. The constant misapplication by people who have used the word instead of 'haven't' and 'isn't' is the reason for the word's fall from grace. If used in its proper place, 'ain't' is no less respectable than any other contraction with which it has become entangled. Actually, the 'well-spoken' person who shuns, for example, 'Ain't I?' in favour of the admittedly more usual 'Aren't I?', is actually the one guilty of atrocious grammar. 'Ain't I?' is standing quite correctly in substitution for 'Am I not?', or the more correct but infinitely clumsy 'Am not I?'. Would the people who insist on the use of 'aren't' feel at ease with 'Are I not?' or even 'Are not I?'?

AIR POCKETS

As a moment's thought will illustrate, there is no such thing; how can there be? There cannot possibly be an isolated partial vacuum just sitting there in the atmosphere. The phenomenon that causes an aeroplane to drop suddenly is really a down-draught of air.

ALASKA

Even if provided with an atlas, most people would staunchly maintain that Maine was the most eastern of the United States, Florida the most southern, and Alaska the most northern and most western. As a matter of fact, Hawaii is the most southern and, ridiculous as it might sound, Alaska is the most northern, western and eastern, all at the same time.

It must be remembered that America is a pretty big country and Alaska does not even start until the 140° meridian, and that's already a long way west of the Californian coast. The Aleutian Islands, which are part of the State of Alaska, extend far beyond the 180° meridian which is the dividing line between the eastern and western hemispheres, therefore, there are parts of Alaska that are many hundreds of miles further east than the eastern coast of America.

AMERICA HAS THE HIGHEST MURDER RATES
Surprisingly enough, America does not lead the field in any of the national or local statistics for what has long appeared to be their greatest participation activity. Cape Town, having forty-three homicides per 100,000 population per annum, far outstrips Chicago (14.5 per), New York (21 per), and Detroit (16.1 per).

When it comes to national overall figures, the Brazilians really show us all up as·squeamish softies by streaking into the lead with a staggering 104 slayings per 100,000 population. This works out to about 370 killings for every day of the year, which makes America's last recorded average of 10.2 per 100,000 population look as if they simply aren't trying.

AMERICAN DECLARATION OF INDEPENDENCE WAS SIGNED ON 4 JULY 1776
The date in the heading was merely the date upon which the final draft of the document was voted on; but it was by no means unanimously approved, and some delegates weren't even present to vote on it anyway.

On that day there were no signatures at all, nor was there ever a solemn mass signing as invariably portrayed by Hollywood, rather a gradual process leading through into August. Several signatures were added years later;

Thomas McKean, for example, didn't get around to signing the thing until 1781. Then there is Robert Livingstone, one of the original five delegates to draft out the document, a task he undertook with Jefferson, Franklin and Adams. He helped draft it; he voted in its favour; he even sat down and framed it, but he never got around to signing it. Lastly, it is also myth that John Hancock's was the first signature. Nobody knows when he signed, or who was the first signatory.

AMERICAN INDIANS AND ALCOHOL

As every devotee of horse operas knows, next to Morris dancing and sheep-rearing, selling whisky to the Indians was the lowest thing a man could do in the West. One whiff of a cork and they were transformed into red devils with a tomahawk in one hand and something unspeakable in the other, intent on raping and murdering anyone they came across – because, as everybody knows, the Red Indian has a very low tolerance of alcohol.

This same piece of rubbish is trotted out about, amongst others, the Eskimos, but it is a simple matter of fact that the Indian's ability to metabolise alcohol is identical to that of Europeans, or indeed any other race. True, the rate of alcoholism amongst Indians is twice the national average, but America must look into its heart and history at the way the indigenous population were and are treated to find the answer to that. Perhaps they have done that and found the answer which is why they prefer to believe the myth.

ANAPHRODISIACS SUCH AS BROMIDE SUPPRESS SEXUAL DESIRE

No doubt the recurring myth that the prison authorities 'put something into the cocoa' has gone a long way to promoting this belief. Just as there is no substance, synthetic or natural, that functions as an aphrodisiac (q.v.), the same holds true for the reverse. There is no drug that works directly and selectively to suppress the sex drive; if there were, sex offenders would be a thing of the past.

ANGEL OF MONS

The story that the heavens sent a host of angelic cavalry who, wielding swords of burnished gold, held back the filthy Hun and thus protected the hard-pressed 3rd and 4th Divisions of the Old Contemptibles, serves as a classic example of how a myth can gather so much momentum that otherwise perfectly honest people end up claiming first-hand experience of events that never were. In the case of the so-called Angels of Mons, such people ended up with egg on their faces when the man who first mentioned the 'phenomenon' publicly announced that he had simply intended his account to be a somewhat purple and extended metaphor, using St George to symbolise the British spirit. All to no avail; the myth was already too popular to be killed off, perhaps for no other reason than it confirmed the idea that God was an Englishman.

Eventually, the man who had quite unintentionally started all the fuss in the first place decided that it was high time he spoke out. Arthur Machen, a Welsh journalist on the London *Evening News* who had something of an obsession with things supernatural, had been given the job of covering the fiasco at Mons. That any British troops had survived was considered a miracle and Machen allowed himself the indulgence of waxing lyrical about 'the Spirit of St George, clad in white and leading a host of angels to hold back the German advance'. He was only writing metaphorically and at no time intended to imply that George had actually appeared.

The Angel of Mons kept a low profile for a few decades, but is back again as strong as ever. Today, any one of a dozen books claiming to explain the inexplicable and unscrew the inscrutable mysteries of the universe, will offer accounts of the day the angels went to war.

THE ANIMALS ENTERED THE ARK TWO BY TWO

Leaving aside any debate on the authenticity of the event itself, it must be pointed out that Genesis 7:2–3 states: 'Of every clean beast thou shalt take to thee by sevens, the male and his female: and of the beasts that are not clean by two, the male and his female. Of fowl also of the air by sevens, male and female, to keep seed alive upon the face of all the earth.'

ANIMALS WILL REJECT THEIR YOUNG AFTER HUMAN INTERFERENCE

It is quite possible that this myth was created by well-intentioned country folk to discourage 'townies' from pestering animal life. No animal, wild or otherwise, will reject its offspring just because it has been handled by, and possibly smells of, humans. This will still hold true even if the young are completely removed for several hours, or days. There is, of course, good reason to leave well alone. Most animals who might appear to be abandoned are nothing of the sort and their cries of distress at being 'saved' will most likely cause mama to emerge from the undergrowth to ask just what you think you are doing. And if mama happens to be a grisly bear or something of that nature, you'd better have some good answers ready.

ANY MAN WHO HATES DOGS AND BABIES CAN'T BE ALL BAD

There seems to be a great deal of confusion as to whether the wording was children / small children / little children, babies or whatever; what is important is that W.C. Fields never uttered this immortal line, it was instead said about him at a dinner given in 1938 to honour the comedian's long career.

The location was the Hollywood Friar's Club and, according to all accounts, the after dinner speeches were dragging on and on. H. Allen Smith is quoted as saying: 'Speakers like Eddie Cantor and Georgie Jassel stood up and let the tears flow down their cheeks until it was almost necessary to club them to the floor to stop them.' With the time approaching two in the morning the MC risked GBH by rising to announce yet another speaker, Leo Rosten, who, sensitive to the atmosphere simply stood up and brought the house down by saying, 'Any man who hates dogs and babies (?) can't be all bad.' Rosten later said that he had no idea that he would be called to speak and that he had made the remark in a total daze. 'It was one of those happy ad libs that God sends you from time to time.'

That has the pleasant ring of humility about it but ad lib it most certainly wasn't, the remark had already been made although not about Fields. In the November 1937 issue of *Harper's*, Cedric Worth quotes another New York journalist, Byron Darnton, as saying about people in general: 'No man who hates dogs and children can be all bad.'

APHRODISIACS

Throughout the ages countless foods, drinks, potions and drugs have laboured under this ridiculous label; even the humble potato enjoyed a brief spell of notoriety as such upon its introduction into Europe, at one time selling for a staggering £250 per pound. Tomatoes too were once thought to raise the beast in us so the Puritans, ever anxious to seal off any avenue of pleasure, spread the story that they were poisonous. This was so successful that people left them alone for over 200 years.

Anyway, the best known 'aphrodisiac', apart from rhinoceros horn, is perhaps Spanish fly, which is made from the wing-sheaths of the common blister beetle. The closest to an aphrodisiac effect that men can achieve with this substance is priapism, or permanent erection which is about as much use as a chocolate teapot since all sensitivity leaves the penis under such conditions. In women it can cause the onset of menstruation, more unpleasant side-effects being vomiting, depression, inflammation of the kidneys and death; quite a few selfish men have actually killed the reluctant objects of their desires with Spanish fly.

In short, far from having an aphrodisiac effect, Spanish fly would put the mockers on a Roman orgy. The quicker that man learns that there just isn't any such thing, the better for all concerned, especially the poor rhinoceros who is still being slaughtered because silly old men think its horn will make them young studs again. There have been a few pseudo-scientific attempts to produce such a substance, the latest being yohimbine, a crystalline alkaloid made from the yohimbe tree of Central Africa – but even that is all bark and no bite.

ARS GRATIA ARTIS

Sam 'Include me out' Goldwyn was called many things in his life but never an aesthete, so it is perhaps not surprising to learn that the above motto as used by MGM is grammatically incorrect. The Latin for 'art for art's sake' (in the movies?) is *ars artis gratia*, but when all the work was completed for the company's lofty new maxim, Goldwyn didn't think that the wording looked

9

properly balanced atop the lion's head and told the art department to shuffle it around to make it look better. There was much shifting from foot to foot as it was put to the great man that such shenanigans were hardly in keeping with the ethos of the statement and that it would be expensive to alter everything at such a late stage. Goldwyn apparently muttered something along the lines of, 'Copulata expensum et ethos, change it.' So, Ars Gratia Artis it is.

ARYANS AS A NORDIC RACE

A. Hitler & Co were responsible for the establishment of this piece of nonsense. They did so much to encourage the fallacy that an Aryan was a strapping Nordic type that this is the very mental image provoked by the word today. Unfortunately for the Nazis, a true Aryan could not be further from this colour scheme if he tried since he has black hair and dark skin.

Aryans first made an appearance in 2000 BC, or thereabouts, when they infiltrated Afghanistan from Central Asia. Some 500 years later they moved into the Punjab and subsequently extended their influence as far as the Ganges and the Vindhya range. The word 'Aryan' was used by early Hindu and Persian peoples to mean 'noble' and, strictly speaking, the only Aryans about today are Iranians and Indians.

The term is also applied to the family of languages which includes Sanskrit, Zend, Persian, Greek, Latin, Teutonic and Slavonic. An alternative name for the group is Indo-Germanic and so, probably due to 'Aryan's' connotations of nobility, Adolph and his Reichstag band hijacked the word, bastardised its meaning and misapplied it in a racial context. In the end, they bandied the term about so much that they robbed it of any meaning at all. They used the word to describe anything or anyone non-Jewish; even the

Japanese were pronounced honorary Aryans after they teamed up with Germany.

ASSAULT AND BATTERY
Assault is a grossly misunderstood and misapplied term. It does not mean to attack someone physically; it is assault merely to threaten or to attempt the use of violence, even if no contact is made. Under the right circumstances just shouting and screaming at another person is sufficient to constitute an assault. The charge of battery is added as soon as physical contact is made. In theory, shouting at someone and then pushing them aside is assault and battery.

AUBURN MEANS REDDY-BROWN
To put it bluntly, 'auburn' means nothing of the sort; it really means white or whitish and, if applied to hair, it means blonde and not reddy-brown. Stemming from the Latin *alburnus*, the term was misunderstood as soon as it arrived here in the form of 'auborne' – most likely due to some confusion with 'broune', which was then the spelling of brown.

AUTOMATIC REPRIEVES FOR SURVIVORS OF UNSUCCESSFUL EXECUTIONS
There has long been a popular notion that anyone who survived a bungled execution is entitled to an automatic reprieve but, although this has happened on compassionate grounds, it has no legal backing. There have been several cases where prisoners have 'come back to life' after being taken down from the gallows, but most were dragged back for an action replay. In 1932, an American murderer named Bullen actually survived Old Sparky and surprised all and sundry by leaping out of

his coffin. He was put back into the chair and left till well done.

You see, the law states that it is the sentence which must be executed (in the sense of 'carried out'), not the condemned man. If the prisoner survives the attempt, then sentence has not been executed. Actually, whilst on the subject of the electric chair, let's dispense with the film-engendered myth that the prison lights dim and flicker every time there is an execution. Quite apart from the fact that it would be sheer lunacy to permit any such thing in the psychological powder-keg of a death-row prison, the chair works by creating a massive short circuit so it is utterly impossible to have the thing linked up to the regular supply without blowing everything in the place. It runs off its own generator.

B

BAGPIPE

The heading is deliberately in the singular since this is the correct form and not the more common but incorrect 'bagpipes'. There may be several drones, but there is only one chanter or pipe.

Despite its now traditional bond with Scotland, the instrument did not originate there but, most likely, in Persia. From there it spread to ancient Rome and Greece after which it arrived here care of the Roman invasion. Actually, some say (and I can hear the claymores rasping in their scabbards even now) that the haggis came in through the same door, the Romans having devised it as marching rations with an acceptable shelf-life.

BALSA IS A SOFTWOOD

The terms 'hardwood' and 'softwood' refer to the two main types of physical structure that you find in timber; they are indications as to the physical make-up of the wood, not whether it is easy or hard to work. Balsa is about the best example of a soft hardwood but, although light, it's not the lightest, as most imagine. The wood of the Aeschynomene Hispada tree of Cuba is the lightest in the world with a specific gravity of 0.044. On the other side of the coin, yew is classed as a softwood even though it is ideal for making, amongst other things, longbows.

BANGKOK IS THE CAPITAL OF THAILAND

Patently impossible since, in reality, there is no such place – not as far as the Thais are concerned at any rate. They call their capital Krung Thep, only foreigners, noticeably Europeans, call the place Bangkok, that being the name of a long-gone village upon whose site King Rama I decided to build his new capital in 1782. Translating as 'The City of the Gods, The Great City, The Residence of the Emerald Buddha, The Impregnable City of Ayutthaya of the God Indra, the grand capital of the world endowed with nine precious stones, the happy city abounding in an enormous Royal Palace which resembles the heavenly abode where reigns the reincarnated god (almost finished), a city given by Indra and built by Vishnukarn', the place's full name is, wait for it, Krungthep Maha Nakorn, Amarn Rattanakosindra, Mahindrayudhya, Mahadilokpop Noparatana Rajdhani Mahasathan, Amorn Piman Avatarn Satit, Sakkatultiva Vishnukarn Prasit, which not only makes Llanfairpwllgwyngyllgogerychwyrndrobwllllantysiliogogogoch look a bit sick, but it also explains why Europeans call the place Bangkok.

THE BATTLE OF WATERLOO WAS WON ON THE PLAYING FIELDS OF ETON

An assertion attributed to the Duke of Wellington, but it is more than doubtful that he ever said any such thing. He had little time for the 'public school spirit' and even less for Eton College itself – the school from which his parents removed him since his lack of academic ability did not justify the expenditure of money they considered better spent on his brothers Gerald and Henry who were brighter pupils. The Duke once made a point of refusing to give so much as sixpence to a collection being made to raise funds to make improvements at the school.

Like all good apocrypha, this did not make an appearance until Wellington had gone to the great battlefield in the sky and was unable to refute the tale. The 'quote' was first seen in 1855 in a book entitled *De L'Avenir Politique de L'Angleterre* (Political Future of England) by Count Charles de Montalembert, and takes the form of 'It is here that the Battle of Waterloo was won' – written as if said by Wellington whilst standing on those hallowed acres. It is this that destroys any credibility in the assertion. When Wellington was at the school there were no playing fields, indeed, there were no organised games at all, and secondly, he only revisited the place once, in 1841, and never left the shelter of the buildings in the short duration of his stay. The whole thing originated in Montalembert's mind as the kind of thing that a Frenchman would imagine an Englishman saying about his alma mater.

BEAVERS – MYTHS SURROUNDING

Probably the most widespread myth attached to the beaver is the notion that it can fell trees exactly where it wants them. Actually, the beaver simply chews away at any old point of the compass since its first interest in the tree is the food value of the bark. The less nimble-footed and astute of the species have been found dead, crushed to death by a snack brought down on their own heads.

Although it is true that some beaver dams do incorporate a curve into the main body of the water, this should not be taken as an indication of any inate comprehension of the laws of stress on behalf of the creature. They build dams in all sorts of shapes and sizes, some just end up in a curve, others in zigzags, and some get swept away.

Lastly, there is the charming idea of the beaver using its broad tail as a trowel to pat down mud into the dam. Although their lives might be made a great deal easier if they did, they do no such thing. They use their tails as rudders when swimming, as a kind of prop when sitting up, or, and this is most probably how the myth got started, as a distress alarm by beating it on the water.

'BECAUSE IT WAS THERE'

This famous reply that Sir Edmund Hillary is supposed to have made to the question: 'Why did you want to climb Everest?' was actually uttered by Mallory who died on his last unsuccessful attempt to conquer the mountain in 1924. Hillary succeeded in 1953 and what he said upon his return was: 'We've knocked the bastard off.' Not quite in the same *Boy's Own* spirit as the other quote, but there it is.

BEELZEBUB IS ANOTHER NAME FOR THE DEVIL

Nothing to do with Old Nick at all, 'Baalzebub', as the deity's name is properly spelt, was actually a god of the ancient Israelites. They in turn had pinched the character from Baal Ekron who was the Philistines' Lord of the Flies.

ST BERNARD DOGS AND THEIR BRANDY CASKS

One of the most popular images of these lovely dogs is that of them setting out to find lost travellers with a tiny cask of brandy slung about their necks. Unfortunately for those who like this romantic image, the monks of the St Bernard Hospice have checked their records back to the early 1600s and can find no reference to their dogs as the original hair thereof. Furthermore, the dogs were never bred or intended for rescue work, their purpose was to help the monks find *their* way about in the snow.

The myth seems to have started at the hands of a Swiss confectionery manufacturer named Lambielle who was producing brandy-flavoured chocolate bars in the early 1900s. Only intended to be an indication as to the flavour, the wrapper showed a St Bernard sitting against a back-drop of the Alps with the now traditional cask about its neck.

SARAH BERNHARDT AND HER WOODEN LEG

She never had anything of the kind! It is true that she had to have a leg amputated at the ripe old age of 72, but she adamantly refused to have an artificial one fitted. She ordered a chair to be made specifically to allow its movement around the narrow passages of theatres and continued to act roles that could be played seated.

THE BIRDMAN OF ALCATRAZ

The popular image of Robert Franklin Stroud, better known as the Birdman of Alcatraz, is that of a gentle, caring old man whiling away his time in a double-sized cell packed with his little feathered friends. The originator of this wholly erroneous impression was the film starring Burt Lancaster.

In 1916, whilst already serving time for murder in Levenworth, Stroud killed a guard during an argument about some trifling matter, and it is quite safe to assume that he was precisely what the authorities locked him away as – a highly dangerous and unpredictable psychopath. In 1920, still in Levenworth, he found four fledgling sparrows in the exercise yard and was allowed to look after them for a short while. He did subsequently become interested in ornithology and read a great deal on the subject, but let's face it, he had plenty of time. He also wrote a couple of books on birds which, according to most, were basically plagerisms of limited merit and, had they not held the novelty factor of having been written by a multiple murderer, it is doubtful that they would ever have seen the light of day.

Twenty-two years later in 1942, Stroud was moved to solitary on Alcatraz because he was once again becoming dangerous and hard to handle. Throughout the next twenty-one years of his life, which ended on The Rock with a massive heart attack on 21 November 1963, he kept no birds at all.

BLACK MAMBAS AND THEIR SPEED OF ATTACK

These snakes are quite rightly feared for their unique ferocity and speed of strike, but stories of their speed over ground are gross exaggerations. No snake can overtake a running man or, even more ridiculously, a galloping horse, as has frequently been claimed for the black mamba. Their strike speed is phenomenal and, unlike other snakes, mambas do not content themselves with just the one bite but strike repeatedly as if in some sort of frenzy. The best turn of speed the snake can muster over ideal terrain is about 7 mph – and the mamba is the fastest snake alive.

BLOOD THINS IN HOT CLIMATES
The blood of Europeans who go to live in, shall we say, Africa, does not 'thin out' to enable them to cope with the heat; the consistency remains exactly the same. Dilution of the blood does occur during heat-stroke, but that's hardly the same thing.

BLOODHOUNDS
This dog is not so called because of its extensive use in tracking down criminals and missing persons, but because it belongs to the breed that first had records kept of its bloodline. The earliest known records were kept by the monks of St Hubert in ninth-century France, but the breed was known as early as the third century in Italy.

BLUE VEINS IN CHEESE
Copper wire implants are usually believed to be responsible for the veining in cheese, whereas the cause is the deliberate introduction of bacteria. Mould spores are mixed in with the curds and, after the cheese has been shaped, it is repeatedly pierced with stainless steel needles. This allows in air to facilitate bacterial growth. Before stainless steel was available, copper needles were used to the same end and, probably due to the fact that copper turns a bluish-green when oxidised, people presumed the copper itself to be somehow responsible for the blue veins.

BOOMERANGS
First to be dispelled is the idea that the name 'boomerang' derived from early settlers asking Australian natives what the device was called, only to be informed 'Boomerang!' which meant 'It has no name!'

Although a native word, it means no such thing and its origins are totally obscure.

Next there is the totally fallacious concept of a boomerang being thrown at an enemy or prey to whom it deals a fatal blow before returning to its owner. Any boomerang thrown with such intent by a thrower skilful enough to predict the weapon's parabolic trajectory with sufficient accuracy to bring it into contact with a moving target, would come to a very sudden stop. Apart from anything else, the returning boomerang is virtually unknown throughout most of Australia where the hunting boomerang is the main weapon. This is a different shape; it travels in a straight line; it is thrown in a completely different way and is absolutely lethal. In areas where the returning variety is known, it is mainly used for fun or sport, although sometimes they are used to throw above low or grounded flights of ducks who, mistaking the boomerang for a hovering hawk, fly in a panic into pre-placed nets.

Although the weapon's links with Australia are indissoluble in the popular mind, it is far from unique to that country. The ancient Egyptians were known to have used them, as did certain peoples of India and Africa; not to mention the American Red Indian.

BRANDY MUST BE SERVED IN SPECIFIC MEASURES IN PUBS

Brandy is a wine derivative and, just as there is no legal measure for wine, there is no legal measure for brandy. It is for this very reason that you will never see brandy included on those little notices that hang behind the bar telling customers what fraction of a gill constitutes a measure in that particular pub. Brandy is always dispensed from an optic, but this is simply a matter of convenience.

It is also worth mentioning here that the number of

stars on a brandy bottle mean absolutely nothing as does the word 'Napoleon', and the letters VSOP. There is no official body issuing or monitoring the usage of such terms which can be used willy-nilly by anybody.

BRANDY SHOULD BE GIVEN TO PEOPLE IN SHOCK

Although people in shock usually complain of a raging thirst, they should not be given anything to drink at all – certainly no alcohol, and there are very good reasons why not. First, the patient needs to be kept warm and, contrary to popular opinion, alcohol actually lowers the body temperature; the warm flush it produces is really the effect of heat leaving the body. Secondly, one of the main problems with shock is the disruption of normal blood supply to the vital organs, and alcohol draws blood away to the skin, hence 'boozer's flush'. Finally, if the state of shock has been induced by a fall or an accident of some kind, you don't know if there are any internal injuries which would hardly be improved by sousing them in spirit.

BRIAR PIPES

More properly the word should be 'brier' for such pipes never have been made out of briar. Originally the word was spelt 'bruyer' since it derived from the French *bruyère*, which was a term applied to heathland but also specifically to the white heath of the Jura, a plant much used in pipe manufacture. It was the atrocious pronunciation of *bruyère* achieved by the English which produced the misconception that the English briar was somehow involved.

BRIDES AND AISLES

No one has ever seen a bride walking down the aisle; not during the wedding ceremony at any rate. The aisles are the passages flanking the central passage, or nave, down which the bride walks.

BROADSWORDS WERE TWO-HANDED WEAPONS

Many are the films in which you can see noble knights hacking away at each other with broadswords gripped with both hands and murderous intent. Doubtless there were occasions when they were employed as such, the final death-blow to a fallen foe, for example, but in standard combat they were a single-handed weapon and were balanced as such.

BUMBLEBEES AND THEIR AERODYNAMIC INFEASIBILITY

When exhorting his luckless minions to attempt the impossible or the insanely suicidal, Hitler is believed to have been fond of quoting Dr Heinkel as saying that the bumblebee was an aerodynamic impossibility but, being ignorant of that drawback, it nevertheless flew. Still today people can be heard slandering the humble bumblebee's right to air space, and pronouncing sagely that no one knows how on earth they fly because they deny all the laws of aerodynamics by getting off the ground.

The short answer to this one is that the bee flies by moving its wings up and down, just like any other member of the living world flying club. If the bumblebee was an aerodynamic impossibility then it wouldn't fly – no matter how ignorant of the facts it was.

C

'C' AND COMMON TIME IN MUSIC

In the early days of music, the tempo that was invariably employed was 3/4 time, or three beats to the bar. This was generally known as 'perfect time', in reference to the Trinity, and the symbol chosen to represent it was a circle. With the advent of the new, trendy 4/4 time, a different symbol had to be found for this 'imperfect time', and a broken circle was considered the most apposite. When 4/4 became more usually called common time, people just assumed the symbol to be a letter 'C'.

'CABAL' AND THE MINISTERS OF CHARLES II

The favourite myth surrounding this word is that it is an acronym formed from the initials of the surnames of a group of conniving ministers at the court of Charles II, they being named Clifford, Ashley, Buckingham, Arlington and Lauderdale. This, however, was purely coincidental and the word has its roots buried much deeper in history and the ancient Hebrew *kabbala*, the secret lore expounded by the rabbis who read hidden meanings into the Bible. Here it was that the word picked up its connotations of secrecy and mystery, this being fuelled by the fact that most races regarded the Jews with more than a little suspicion. The word fell from common usage until 1670 when, due to the convenient initials of the aforementioned ministers, it re-emerged with all its current overtones.

CAESAR WAS A ROMAN EMPEROR ASSASSINATED IN THE CAPITOL

He was dictator of Rome four times but never Emperor. There was a very simple reason for this; the Roman Empire wasn't founded until 27 BC which was seventeen years after his death.

Perhaps William Shakespeare has done more than most to foster the idea that Caesar was bumped off in the Capitol, whereas he was really killed at the foot of a statue of Pompey in a room sometimes used as a meeting place by the Senate. As for his having uttered the famous 'Et tu, Brute?', it is more than doubtful that he said any such thing. Suetonius, the Roman historian, recording the events shortly after wrote: 'Caesar did not utter a sound after Casca's blow had drawn a groan from him' – and Casca struck first.

CAESARIAN SECTION AND JULIUS CAESAR

According to some, the first caesarian section that was successful for both mother and child occurred in 1500 when Jacob Nufer, a pig gelder of Sigershauffen in Switzerland, conducted such an operation on his wife using the tool of his trade. A long shadow of doubt is cast over this event by the fact that good old Frau Nufer went on to have six more children by normal delivery. It must be remembered that cleanliness was only next to godliness in an Irish dictionary in the 1500s, and the standard of attendant hygiene as a man hacked away at his other half with a gelding knife makes survival highly unlikely and further successful pregnancies nothing short of a miracle. More conservative medical opinion prefers the 1738 operation executed by a midwife in Charlemont, Ireland, since the mother was available for examination afterwards.

Many ancient cultures had a taboo about burying a woman with a child inside her; it was required to be cut out and buried separately. In ancient Rome this was called the Lex Caesaria, and was so called from *caesus*, the past participle of *caedere* which meant to cut. Thus it was performed on dead women in Rome and Caesar's mother is known to have been alive when he began his little tour of the British Isles. It is possible that a child might survive a short time if so extracted from its mother immediately after her death, providing that birth was imminent anyway, but it is highly unlikely. It must be remembered that it is only very recently that the operation has achieved the tag 'routine', and had anyone as famous as Caesar been so delivered and had his mother survived the ordeal, much would have been made of it – intervention of the gods and all that – yet no reference is made to the manner of his birth during his lifetime.

More telling than anything is the fact that Julius was not the first of his family to bear the name Caesar. It is indeed a strange anachronism if Julius was named for the fact that he was 'cut from his mother's womb' as Pliny the Elder would have us believe, or that the operation was subsequently named after him. One of his ancestors was Lucius Julius Caesar, a one time consul of Rome, and it could well be that Julius was simply named after him.

CAJUN

On our side of the Atlantic, this term is mistakenly thought to refer to those people of the southern States of America who are of mixed blood or of Red Indian descent. In fact, it refers exclusively to white people.

Some time around 1775, when the French and British were merrily slaughtering each other for the possession of Canada, the British rounded up all the French settlers from an area known as Arcadia and drove them out as possible fifth columnists. These people eventually settled in Louisiana where they were first known as Cadians, and then Cajuns.

CALIGULA MADE HIS HORSE A CONSUL
Caligula was without doubt one of the least liberal and balanced of the Emperors tolerated by Rome, but he never made his horse, Incitatus, a priest and consul of the city. That the animal was pampered to the point of ill-treatment is beyond dispute, but things didn't go quite as far as most of the stories maintain. This is not to say that the man wasn't looney enough to do such a thing, perhaps it simply never occurred to him.

CAMELS – MYTHS SURROUNDING
Perhaps it is not altogether surprising that such an extraordinary creature should find itself the subject of so many myths and fallacies. Surely it is no longer necessary to state that the camel does not store water in its hump, for one would hope that that old chestnut is firmly laid to rest. To be fair, there was by coincidence some indirect truth in the myth for, when the fat that was stored in the hump was called upon as food reserve, some water was produced in subsequent digestion.

The camel does store water but does so in its stomach which is lined with pouches that fill up when the animal guzzles its formidable quantities – as much as thirty gallons at one time. The water is retained by a sphincter muscle and conserved because the camel's temperature can shoot up to the early hundreds before it even begins to sweat, it also urinates very infrequently.

There is, however, no chance for the camel to escape from the grip of myth, for its parsimonious use of water has given birth to yet more fallacies about its ability to survive without it. Suggestions of several weeks are absolutely ridiculous. A fully laden camel in desert conditions can go for three, possibly four, days without fresh water, but no more. Any assertions to the contrary are at best confused with the animal's capability under 'winter' conditions when, unladen, it can survive for as long as seventeen to twenty days without drinking.

The camel is far from being a leader in the 'no water' stakes. The giraffe can go for months without drinking since it derives most of its moisture from its diet; the same goes for certain species of antelope.

CARROTS IMPROVE THE EYESIGHT

A Second World War RAF programme started the tales about carrots and eyesight. The RAF did conduct some limited experiments to see if carrots would improve night vision since they do contain vitamin A which is thought to have links with visual accuracy, in that it aids the production of visual purple, a pigment in the retina essential to good vision in restricted light. The programme produced no conclusive results and was dropped. Later, in the early days of radar, which was all very hush-hush, stories began circulating that the experiments had been a complete success which explained the apparent ease with which British fighters were finding enemy planes in the dark.

CATGUT

Quite why we persist in calling this substance catgut is obscure since it never has been made from the intestines of cats but from those of sheep or horses. A possible explanation for the mistake is that an old word for a small fiddle was 'kit', another is that people once wrongly thought the intestines of cattle to be involved.

CATHOLIC PRIESTS AND MARRIAGE

It is quite true that, once ordained, for a priest of the Roman Catholic Church marriage is out of the question, as indeed are sexual relationships of any shape or form. Historically, this has never bothered innumerable popes, cardinals and priests, not to mention nuns found running virtual brothels, but that's another matter. It is not, however, impossible to have a married Catholic priest – there are quite a few scattered around the globe.

Should a priest of another persuasion decide to shift his allegiance to the Vatican, his marital status will by no means prevent his being welcomed into the Roman Catholic Church and being ordained.

CELERY AS A NEGATIVE FOOD

Sometimes the apple too is saddled with this ridiculous label, meaning that the body burns up more calories in the physical effort of eating such foods than it derives from the consumption thereof. This myth might afford some comfort to slimmers, but that's about the extent of it.

The human body uses up about 0.3 of a calorie per minute whilst eating. This means that a stick of celery containing but six calories would need to be chewed for about twenty minutes to make the above myth come to life.

CELTS ARE SHORT, DARK AND WIRY

Just as the popular image of the typical Aryan is the exact opposite of the reality, the above description of a Celt is a complete misconception.

The Celts can be divided into two broad categories. The first is that of the Celts of north-western Europe who are the people more usually referred to as Nordic. They have their main seat in Scandinavia and being tall, well built, with blonde hair and blue eyes, they conform to the misconstrued concept of the typical Aryan. The second group, sometimes called the Alpine Celts due to their prevalence along the mountain chains of south-western France, Switzerland and the Tirol, were of normal stature, if a trifle broad, and had hazel grey eyes and light coloured hair.

It has been mooted that the abundance of short, dark people in the areas of England and Wales that are presumed to have been Celtic strongholds is due to extensive interbreeding with visiting Mediterranean traders and sailors. Whether this be true or no, Celts in our neck of the woods were big, strapping blondes.

CHAMELEONS CAN CHANGE COLOUR TO SUIT THE BACKGROUND

It may be true that these creatures can be observed going through some mild colour changes, but this is not a deliberate attempt at camouflage on their behalf. Such colour change as does take place is caused by disperse-ment or concentration of pigments at the instigation of the autonomic nervous system which, in turn, is triggered by light, temperature or emotional condition. Fright, for example, will promote a colour change, but if you crept up behind a chameleon and shouted 'Boo!', it would always turn the same colour no matter how many times you changed its environment.

CHEETAHS AND THEIR FLEETNESS OF FOOT

Perhaps eventually tiring of uninspiring tales of a cat that could only manage a paltry 60 mph, the popular imagination went to work on the already incredible prowess of the cheetah. Laughable and completely unsub-stantiated claims of 90 mph plus have been put forward, but anything over 65 mph should be studiously ignored.

Nor is the cheetah anything like the fastest creature alive; the real speed merchants belong in the sky. The white-throated spinetail swift on level flight has been clocked at 106.2 mph, and the peregrine falcon often exceeds 200 mph in stoops, or strike-dives.

CHOP SUEY AS AN AMERICAN DISH

Many people, notably Americans, love to pronounce this to be true, but chop suey is exactly what it sounds – Chinese. True it first made an appearance in the States, but did so in the Chinese labour camps of the railroads and the like. The coolie labourer was not exactly overburdened with good food and high wages and was forced to do the best he could with what was made available to him. Meaning 'various things', chop suey described an anything-goes dish in which the only American influence was the fact that the Chinese cooks had to use local produce, not having any bamboo shoots, etc.

So, chop suey was developed by Chinese, cooked by Chinese and eaten by Chinese, they just happened to be in America at the time. If the cure for cancer was discovered by American scientists who were working in China, would the White House announce it as a Chinese breakthrough? I think not.

CHRISTIANS WERE TOSSED TO THE LIONS IN THE COLOSSEUM

Certainly common criminals and other condemned men were thrown to assorted wild animals in the Colosseum, but never Christians. Nor did Nero ever preside over the gory spectacles that took place there because the arena didn't open until AD 80, which was twelve years after Nero brightened everybody's day by doing away with his repugnant self. This is not to say that Nero didn't take a very active and personal hand in the brutal mass murder of Christians as a sick floorshow in his own private gardens during parties. There are extant records of his having some Christians clad in animal skins to be torn to pieces by dogs whilst others were crucified and set on fire to illuminate the nightmare. In fact, whenever specific animals are mentioned, instead of just 'wild beasts', it is almost invariably dogs that are involved, lions seem to be a figment of more recent imagination.

To return to the Colosseum, during the sixteenth and seventeenth centuries the Colosseum was plundered not only of its fine marble seating and statues, but of its very masonry. To put a stop to this, Pope Benedict XIV declared the place to be ground consecrated to the blood of Christians martyred there. Benedict was well aware that no such persecutions had taken place, he simply wanted to stop the pilfering. Since the main ramification of his edict was that, overnight, removing stones suddenly became an iconoclastic act tantamount to heresy and therefore punishable by various unpleasant modes of execution, the thefts came to a rapid halt.

Despite its name and reputation, the Colosseum was not the largest of the ancient stadiums – holding a modest 45,000 at best, it was not even large by today's standards. Dwarfing the Colosseum and the largest of the modern stadiums was the Circus Maximus which was constructed several centuries before the Colosseum and which accommodated upwards of 300,000. The largest of the contemporary stadiums is the Strahov in Prague which holds but a modest 240,000. You see, the Colosseum wasn't so named because it was big, but because it was built near the Colossus of Nero in the Via Sacra.

CHRONIC MEANS SEVERE

It means nothing of the sort, it simply means lasting a long time and shares a common root with chronology and chronicle. A grossly misused word, 'chronic' is bandied about as if it means 'terrible', 'awful', or as in the case of illness, 'severe'. A protracted state of elation or life-long contentment could quite legitimately be described as chronic happiness.

CIRCUMSTANTIAL EVIDENCE

In popular parlance the above designation is most often used in a way that indicates a widespread misconception as to its real meaning. 'Circumstantial' does not mean weak, flimsy or coincidental, yet time and again one hears thin evidence backing up unsubstantiated accusations being dismissed out of hand as 'purely. circumstantial'. Every such use reinforces the myth that 'circumstantial' and 'coincidental' are somehow synonymous in this context.

Any evidence presented in court which is not an eye witness account is properly designated as circumstantial, i.e. arising from the facts and circumstances of the case or crime. If there is one form of evidence that is notoriously contradictory and liable to change from day to day with each telling, it is eye witness account, not circumstantial evidence. The invariably irrefutable forensic evidence that proves that the suspect was on the murder scene at the right time, that his skin and blood were found under the victim's fingernails, that the victim was killed with a particular blunt instrument that was later found in the suspect's possession, is properly described as circumstantial evidence. 'Circumstantiate' is still used to mean corroborate and substantiate beyond any reasonable doubt.

CIRRHOSIS OF THE LIVER IS CAUSED BY ALCOHOLISM

Alcohol is a slow poison, but its excessive consumption is not the cause of cirrhosis of the liver which, incidentally, is not the only anatomical location that the condition can strike. Cirrhosis of the liver is basically a form of acute malnutrition caused by protein deficiency; it is only common amongst alcoholics because they ignore food in favour of drink to avoid all that tedious chewing. The disease is endemic to renowned famine areas, the inhabitants of which drink no alcohol at all.

CLEOPATRA – HER NEEDLES AND HER SUICIDE

The monument that stands on the Thames Embankment has no connection with Cleopatra and the erroneous connection has never been properly explained – apart from the fact that the needle did come from Egypt and, as far as the West is concerned, Cleopatra was that country's most famous character. Along with its twin, the monument was erected at Heliopolis some time around 1500 BC which was 1,500 years before Cleopatra put in an appearance. They were moved to Alexandria where they stayed until 1877 when one went to New York and the other to London.

So much for the needle, and on to the lady herself. By the time of her birth in 68 BC, her name was already the recognised title for Queens of Egypt; there were several Cleopatras, the lady in question being the daughter of Ptolemy XI. Actually, Cleopatra, like the rest of her line, was of Greek and not Egyptian descent since the first Ptolemy was the son of Lagos, a general in the army of Alexander the Great. He seized power in Egypt and made himself king.

Next we have her tender disposition towards Mark Antony which is best left to Shakespeare who was never one to let fact and credibility stand in the way of a good story. After their joint defeat at Actium by Octavian, Cleopatra readily accepted the victor's proposal to do away with Mark Antony as a means of saving herself and her position. She summoned her lover to the mausoleum already built for the pair of them, and there convinced him that she had already taken poison. Mark Antony promptly did the gentlemanly thing and ran himself through with his sword. This securing of Antony's death was the mainstay of a deal struck with Octavian whereby she could remain as ruler of Egypt but answerable to Rome. It was only when she learnt that Octavian really intended to take her back to Rome and parade her through the streets that she resolved to kill herself. Hardly the tender love-pact of popular imagination.

To effect this end, she did not indulge in any high-jinks with a snake of any description. It is worth mentioning here that the snake we call an asp is not and never has been native to Egypt, so she wouldn't have had one lying about. All contemporary accounts state that there was not a single mark on her body, and a snake bite, especially in the tender area of the female breast, would hardly have gone unnoticed. The true facts of the matter must remain a subject for speculation and conjecture but it is highly likely that she killed herself with poison from a bodkin which she habitually wore in her hair. Plutarch seems to have been the originator of all the silly stories about snakes although he is careful never to state such as fact. Peeved at not having the real thing to flaunt in triumph, Octavian had a statue made of Cleopatra to parade through Rome, and this statue had a cobra, the Egyptian royal symbol, wrapped about one arm with the head near the breast. Plutarch, and many others, drew inspiration from as little as that.

COFFEE SOBERS YOU UP

I'm afraid that it does no such thing, and it is a potentially lethal misconception to think otherwise. Once alcohol has entered the bloodstream there is only one thing that will get it out or neutralise it and that is time. Outside the psychological, the only sobering effect produced by coffee is the time it takes to sit down and drink it.

COLD CONDITIONS CAUSE COLDS

If this most persistent of all old wives' tales were true, Eskimos and other inhabitants of inclement climes would suffer from one cold after another all their lives, and just the reverse is true. The common cold is caused by the virus *coryza* and, as with all viruses, its virulence is inhibited by severely cold conditions. Although an extremely uncomfortable and silly thing to do, sitting around in wet clothes will no more cause a cold than it will typhoid.

THE COLOSSUS OF RHODES STOOD ASTRIDE THE HARBOUR ENTRANCE

This statue was far from being the most durable of the Seven Wonders of the Ancient World, it was probably due to the above misconception that it ever gained membership to that élite club. The statue, which took twelve years to build, was the work of Chares of Lindos and measured a mere 117 feet, despite lunatic assertions to the contrary. After standing *beside* the harbour entrance for a mere fifty-six years, it fell down in an earthquake in 224 BC. It was subsequently sold as scrap to a Jew from Emesa who carried it all away on 900 camels.

CONDORS ARE THE LARGEST OF ALL BIRDS

The size, prowess and wingspan of the Andean condor are nothing like as impressive as most imagine. Leaving aside such unfair competition as the ostrich and restricting the field to flying birds alone, the condor, tipping the scales at around the 20-lb mark and measuring in the region of 4 feet, is heavily outgunned by various birds.

It is difficult to understand why the *Encyclopedia Britannica*, to name but one, insists on bestowing the accolade of 'largest flying bird' upon the vulturine head of the condor. The largest wingspan ever recorded was that of a maribou stork in excess of 13 feet which, in a species that rarely exceeds 9½ feet, was admittedly something of a one-off. Weighing the same as the condor, the wandering albatross is the bird with the largest wingspan and, even ignoring the odd rogue specimen taped at a fraction short of 12 feet, the albatross usually averages a comfortable 2 feet in excess of the condor's 9-foot span.

On the domestic front, we have the swan. An impressive bird by any standards, the mute swan usually exceeds 5 feet in length and weighs in excess of 40 lb, which leaves the condor the dubious honour of being the heaviest of all raptors.

COOK DISCOVERED AUSTRALIA

A peculiar form of colour prejudice seems to crop up whenever reference books talk about who was the first to discover wherever. The Chinese knew about Australia in the thirteenth century and talked of the continent to Marco Polo who mentions as much in his writings. The Malays were always popping across to the north coast of Australia but, since they weren't European, they don't seem to count. Even sticking to Europeans, Cook comes a long way down the list and it is hardly accurate to use the term 'discovery' in connection with his famous voyage since he was given all the details and actually sent to Australia.

The French and Portuguese make the odd unsubstantiated claim on behalf of various sixteenth-century explorers but the 1605 sighting of the Australian mainland by de Torres is generally held to have been the first. The first landing came a few months later when, in March 1606, some of the crew of the Dutch ship *Duyfken* went ashore at Cape Keerweer. Thus Captain Jansz of the *Duyfken* can claim to be the true discoverer of Australia. Throughout the next half-century, the Dutch were all over Australia, charting, mapping, and calling the continent New Holland.

The first Englishman to start snooping around was a pirate/navigator named William Dampier who came on the scene in 1688. He returned to England and reported his findings which resulted in his being packed off back down under in 1699 with instructions to investigate further. This he did, exploring some 900 miles of coast from Shark's Bay to Roebuck's Bay. It was nearly a century later in 1768 that Cook was sent to have a good look around, so quite how he grabs the limelight and the credit is a mystery.

COPERNICUS AS THE FATHER OF MODERN ASTRONOMY

Why Copernicus should always be so regarded is obscure, because most of the ideas published in his *De Revolutionibus Orbitum Coelestium* were not only very old hat and orthodox, but, more importantly, they were wrong. He still went along unquestioningly with all the old theories – the planets had perfectly circular orbits, and so forth. His one correct statement that caused all the fuss, namely that the earth moved about the sun and not vice versa, was hardly novel it having been first aired nearly 2,000 years before Copernicus was born.

Aristarchus of Samos (?310–250 BC) first mooted his ideas *c*.279 BC. Not only did he state that the earth moved about the sun, but he also said that the earth itself spun which accounted for the change from day to night. Not content with that, he also wrote that the earth altered on its axis throughout the span of one year and that it was this shift that was responsible for the changing seasons.

Having told everybody that God had created the earth, the Church had no choice except to keep insisting that the earth was the centre of the universe and that everything revolved around it. No one with any knowledge took them seriously, but with the Vatican capriciously incinerating anyone who failed to agree with their edicts, Copernicus took the wise precaution of not publishing his innocuous little dissertation until 1543, by which time he was sure that he was headed for the last place in which cardinals could get their murderous hands on him. Popular belief has it that the first copy was presented to him on his death-bed, but he was well and truly dead before the printing began.

CREOLE

As with Cajun (q.v.), this word is completely misunderstood by most English people. Creole properly applies to white people, specifically those of pure Spanish blood raised in the West Indies. Perhaps the most famous Creole in history was Josephine of 'Not tonight!' fame, she had no mixed blood but was brought up in Martinique.

The word has been hijacked by many races and then misapplied. Its incorrect use in America to describe someone of mixed black and French or Spanish blood has gone most of the way to creating the modern misunderstanding of the term.

D

DEATH CAN BE ESTABLISHED BY LOOKING INTO THE EYES

I'd love to have a pound for every time I've seen an actor lifting the eyelid of some supine character before pronouncing him to be dead. This is nothing but theatricals; no one, and that includes the medical profession, can ascertain whether or not life is present by such a method. The position of the eyes in their sockets is totally irrelevant in such situations, even people who are merely unconscious can often have their eyes rolled back so that only the whites are visible, but they are nevertheless alive.

DEATH SENTENCE HAS BEEN ABOLISHED IN THIS COUNTRY

This simply isn't so. It may have been abolished in respect of murder, but it is still enforceable for certain acts of treason, piracy with violence, and sexual assault on certain members of the Royal Family, but in this last category, considering the members listed, a plea of insanity is a racing certainty. Until 1971, when the law was changed by the Criminal Damages Act, arson in a Navy dockyard also carried the death penalty.

Funnily enough, the 1969 ban was not the first seen in this country. Remarkably liberal for his day, William I abolished capital punishment but it was soon reinstated by Henry I. The only people wholly exempt from the gibbet in England are pregnant women.

'DEMISE' MEANS 'DEATH'

It is nearly always used in that context, but it has no such meaning in real terms. With actual meanings of to give, grant, transfer or convey by means of a will or lease, the word's misunderstanding seems to have been occasioned by its use to describe the transfer of the crown due to the death of the monarch. When people talk about 'the demise of the crown', or whatever, they mean the transfer of the mantle of responsibility, not the death of the crowned head that brought such about.

DENTISTS DRILL INTO THE NERVE

When you feel that unpleasant twinge as some licensed sadist drills a hole in your head, he has not 'hit a nerve' – if he had you would *really* know all about it, anaesthetic or no anaesthetic. Unless you have unwisely bounced a cheque on him, the dentist only drills into the nerve if both it and the tooth are dead, and a dead nerve gives no pain.

'DESIDERATA' WAS PENNED BY AN UNKNOWN ANCIENT

It was the short-lived heyday of the Hippies that swept 'Desiderata' (Go placidly amidst the haste and noise, etc.) along on a wave of posters and wall-hangings. And why not, if everyone lived according to its sentiments the munitions factories would be out of business overnight. Unfortunately for 'Desiderata's' author, there was also a revival of the tale that the piece was one of great antiquity, discovered in Old St Paul's Church, Baltimore, County Cork, and dated to the mid–late 1600s. One would have thought that the modernity of the phrase-ology ('With all its sham, drudgery and broken dreams, it's still a beautiful world. Be careful. Strive to be happy.') would have squashed such a notion flat at the very outset, but in fact many people were actually producing and selling unlicensed reproductions of the work in the genuine belief that it was long out of copyright. But there was copyright, and there still is.

The piece was written by Max Ehrmann who first registered his copyright in 1927. This was renewed by Bertha Ehrmann in 1954 and is still valid today.

DEVIL'S ISLAND WAS A HARD-LINE PENAL COLONY

Of the 70,000 convicts that France shipped out to her penal colonies on the islands of Royale and St Joseph, which were located just off the coast of French Guiana, only 2,000 ever survived their terms of sentence and made it home to France. In stark contrast, conditions on Devil's Island were far from horrific, in fact, by comparison, the place was a regular paradise.

The island, named for the hazardous waters surrounding it rather than for anything diabolical that happened there, is less than one square mile in area, so it would have been quite impossible for it to have accommodated anything like the numbers supposedly imprisoned there. In reality the island held on average about a dozen or so men, this number rising to nearer twenty on rare occasions. All prisoners had their own cabins and were allowed to retain personal possessions. To supplement their diet they grew their own vegetables, harvested the coconuts and went fishing. Mail, parcels from relatives and visiting doctors came regularly by boat and, all in all, life was pretty tolerable.

The reason for all this privilege and comparative luxury was not humanitarian but the fact that all prisoners incarcerated there were of strictly political category and, whether they like it or not, sensible governments look after such men to avoid giving martyrs to the opposition and attracting bad press to themselves. Dreyfus, the French–Jewish army officer framed on charges of treason by his own High Command, was the very first man sent there, in fact, the place was opened up to accommodate him.

The above is just one of the things that casts a long, dark shadow of doubt across the pages of Henri Charriere's *Papillion* which many believe to be nothing more than a good yarn. Significantly, when Alan Wicker produced a documentary on the old colonies he spoke to many people who were around in those days, including those on the mainland who used to help the convicts who did manage to get away, and nobody remembered anyone like Papillion.

DIOGENES LIVED IN A BARREL
That the man was a Cynic seems to be beyond dispute, but he never did anything quite as ridiculous as setting up home in a tub. Actually, it was Seneca, Diogenes' biographer, who was inadvertently responsible for the birth of the whole silly notion. When discussing the man's personal habits, Seneca wrote: 'a man so crabbed ought to have lived in a tub like a dog'. Before long, lots of publications were stating that Diogenes *had* lived in a tub and cited Seneca as their authority.

DIXIELAND IS NAMED FROM THE MASON–DIXON LINE
Oddly enough, even though Dixieland does lie south of the Mason–Dixon line in America, this is but pure coincidence and the name Dixon has nothing to do with 'Dixie'.

During the 1830s, there was so much counterfeit money in circulation in the States that people were quite rightly sceptical of anything other than coins of gold and silver. In an effort to combat this the Citizen's Bank and

41

Trust Company of New Orleans began issuing some highly elaborate notes printed in a mixture of French and English on highly distinctive paper. These notes were an unattractive proposition to the forgers and thus became popular in business circles. The first note issued was a ten dollar bill which had the French 'Dix' printed on the back. Overnight, New Orleans became known as 'Dixie Town', and then the tag spread to embrace the South in general.

DOCK LEAVES RELIEVE NETTLE STINGS

No doubt the belief in this nature cure has been reinforced over the years by the supposed aphorism that anything harmful is always found growing next to its own antidote, and nettles and dock are common neighbours.

Nettle stings are caused by formic acid and there is nothing in the chemical structure of the dock leaf that is going to have the slightest curative effect. It may feel cool and soothing to hold a dock leaf against the effected area, but the same would hold true for any leaf of similar texture.

DODOS WERE HUNTED INTO EXTINCTION

The tale that the dodo was so tasty and easy to catch that they were eaten into history by early explorers of the Mauritius Islands has no foundation at all. In fact, the Dutch sailors called them *walgvogels*, or nauseous bird, since no amount or method of cooking would render them palatable.

Being a flightless bird, their lot was not much improved by the introduction of alien species like cats and dogs who were not quite so fussy about their food as were the Dutch. But at the end of the day, it was the dodo's own cataclysmic stupidity that was its greatest single enemy. The female laid but one egg per year and there was a high infertility rate to boot. Not being overburdened with intelligence, the bird often wandered away from the incubation site and subsequently forgot its location, a trait unlikely to ensure the survival of the species. Although man's stupidity and greed have been responsible for the disappearance of many a species of wildlife, it is fair to say that, sooner or later, the dodo would have waddled off into eternity and forgotten to return without any help from him.

DRINKING ALCOHOL THROUGH A STRAW ACCELERATES DRUNKENNESS

Why some people choose to believe that an alcohol drink magically increases in potency if passed through a narrow tube is puzzling to say the least. The only factors dictating how quickly and severely the drink affects you are age, sex, size, stomach content prior to drinking, acquired tolerance and, to a lesser extent, your emotional state at the time. How and what you consume the alcohol from is totally irrelevant. The reason that sex is included in the list of factors is that women are more affected by alcohol than men. Ingested alcohol is distributed throughout the body's fluid which in men constitutes between 55 per cent and 60 per cent of the total body weight. In women this figure drops to between 45 per cent and 55 per cent, the alcohol thereby being that little bit more concentrated.

Just one more thing, you can safely ignore anyone who comes out with the old rubbish that he can drink whisky all night but two gins, or whatever, and he's out of his tree. This may make a reasonable excuse for having made an utter burke of yourself, but booze, is booze, is booze – the flavour and colour is immaterial; once you've taken on board your own personal limit of the drug $CH OH_2$, be it flavoured of juniper or peppermint, the effect is all the same at the end of the day.

DRINKING MILK LINES THE STOMACH AGAINST ALCOHOL
Yet another load of old tosh. The human stomach is constantly in motion, so nothing can possibly line it. Also, to prevent the embarrassment of our making a meal out of ourselves (the gastric juices can dissolve some metals) the stomach lining is being renewed at the rate of 500,000 cells per minute so, by the time that you get to the pub and start drinking, you haven't even got the same stomach lining. If you don't want to get drunk, don't drink to excess.

DROIT DE SEIGNEUR
The enforcement of the so-called right of the first night has been included in many a medieval romp; in Charlton Heston's 'The Warlord' the whole plot rested on the fatal ramifications, so to speak, of his having done so. Alas for the real barons and warlords of old, there were never any such customs. Any reference to it in ancient documents indicate that no one took it seriously even then. Sometimes a tongue-in-cheek ritual was enacted during which the groom paid a nominal token to his Lord to forego a 'right' that could not be enforced in any case.

DYNAMITE AND NITRO-GLYCERINE
It was not Alfred Nobel but Ascanio Sobrero who developed nitro-glycerine as far back as 1846, but it was not a safe or stable prospect until 1864 when Nobel amalgamated it with a kind of porous silicon dioxide called kieslguhr to produce dynamite.

So stable is dynamite that it requires percussion to set it off, simply raising its temperature is not going to produce any results for quite some time. The familiar scene in Westerns and the like when men scatter as cases of dynamite catch fire and detonate almost immediately, is pure fiction. Heating up sticks of the explosive, even in a live flame, only makes them more sensitive to the blasting cap but will not cause detonation. In fact, in the logging camps of yesteryear in the northern tracts of the North American continent, several sticks of the stuff were set to cook at the same time as breakfast to make sure it would be ready for use first thing. It could have brought a whole new meaning to having bangers for breakfast!

E

EARTHWORMS AND THEIR REGENERATIVE POWERS

Many an unfortunate worm has been unceremoniously hacked to pieces by dilettante vivisectionists attempting to verify the exaggerated tales of the creature's ability to grow into two or more whole creatures after being butchered. They can't.

No matter how many sections are removed from a worm, it can only reproduce about half a dozen, so in the case of a bisected worm the tail half has got no chance of growing a new front inclusive of a head and therefore dies. The front half produces a few segments to 'seal' itself up and survives in an abbreviated form. If a worm's head is severed it can only grow a new one providing the cut is not inflicted further back than about the fifteenth segment in which case the entire creature will die.

EARTHQUAKES AND THE GROUND OPENING UP

Any disaster movie that stars an earthquake feels obliged, for reasons of effect rather than accuracy, to include scenes of racing, yawning tears in the earth that rip across the screen swallowing up people, cars, buildings and anything else in their voracious path. Earthquakes are quite bad enough without this sort of thing happening.

Although it *can* happen, it is very rare indeed and, when it does occur, it is never with the rapidity or on the scale that you tend to see in films. In the 1948 Fukui disaster in Japan one woman is said to have died in such an unpleasant manner and during the 1906 San Francisco quake a cow was similarly despatched. Neither were killed by the ground closing in on them like a giant vice which is something that cannot possibly happen, both died as a result of suffocation caused by surrounding earth collapsing in on them. In the case of the cow, it seems far more likely that it ran in blind panic into a man-made ditch which subsequently collapsed and killed it.

EGYPTIANS WERE POSSESSED OF SUPERIOR SKILLS IN EMBALMING

Many cultures, including European ones, practised the embalming of bodies, but it would be wrong to believe that the remarkable state of preservation of Egyptian mummies indicates any great secret skills now lost in the mists of time. The two main factors responsible were the extremely dry climate and the near non-presence of bacteria in the sand and air. As soon as they are untombed, mummies must be kept in bacteria free, hermetically sealed display cases, or that which has stood against the ravages of thousands of years would fall to prey and pieces because of twentieth-century atmospheric pollution.

ELEPHANTS – THEIR MEMORIES, LONGEVITY AND GESTATION PERIODS

If there are two things that everybody knows about elephants, these are that the animal never forgets and that it has the longest gestation period of any living animal.

Whilst they don't have bad memories, there's nothing particularly remarkable about them either, nor is the animal particularly intelligent. Admittedly they can be taught certain basic work functions and even the odd trick, but nothing as complicated as, for example, the ordinary working routine of a sheepdog. They may remember things for a long time but this is only because they tend to live a long time. The elephant's memory is no better than that of any other animal with a proportionately sized brain.

As to their longevity, all the outlandish claims of 100 years plus can safely be ignored. The *Guinness Book of Records* recognises the current record holder to be a cow named Modoc who died aged 78 in California in 1975. It is man who, with the exception of certain species of tortoise and the quahog, outlives every animal on the planet – both on land and in the sea.

With regard to the gestation period of an elephant, it may be the longest of any mammal but, at an average of 609 days, it is a long way behind the alpine black salamander which can take up to 1,140 days to produce results.

EPOCH

Current usage, or rather misuse, has corrupted the meaning of this word to mean an era or a span of years covering related events, whereas it actually means a specific point in time. We took the word from Greek where it meant a stop or pause. In proper terms, an era begins and ends with an epoch.

47

EROICA SYMPHONY AND ITS DEDICATION TO NAPOLEON

It is true that Beethoven originally intended to call this work 'Bonaparte' but later changed the title to 'Heroic Symphony – composed to celebrate the memory of a great man.' Whether or not Napoleon's move to declare himself hereditary Emperor influenced this decision is by no means certain; many dispute the tale and Beethoven himself repeatedly referred to the piece as actually being dedicated to and named for Napoleon long after the relevant proclamation. Either way, there is absolutely no truth whatsoever in the tale that Beethoven, upon hearing the news, burst into tears and ripped up the title page of the composition in a tantrum. The original page is still extant and simply shows Bonaparte's name neatly crossed out.

ESKIMOS AND IGLOOS

The igloo is not and never has been the Eskimo's standard residence. In fact, the ice dome construction was never universal to the Eskimo people; only those who lived between the delta of the MacKenzie river and Labrador built them, and even there they are considered a trifle passé; apart from anything else, there's nowhere to plug in the television. A relatively recent survey conducted amongst about 4,000 Eskimos showed that under 2 per cent had ever even seen an igloo, let alone been inside one.

In the Eskimo language, the word *iglu* does not refer specifically to the ice house, the word simply means 'house' and can be applied to any structure intended for residence. That which we call an igloo is merely a temporary shelter used when the Eskimo is on the move. They can be constructed with incredible speed and are abandoned when no longer required.

ETHELRED THE UNREADY
The epithet 'Unready' in no way implies that Ethelred was in some way caught napping by events. The word should be spelt 'Unrede' which means without council or advice. It seems that the headstrong young chap repeatedly chose to ignore the advice of the Witenagemot, which was a sort of Anglo-Saxon think-tank-cum-National Assembly. Somewhat miffed by Ethelred's scant regard for their grey-haired sagicity, it was the Witenagemot that most likely gave him the nickname.

EUNUCHS ARE INCAPABLE OF SEXUAL UNION
As many a lady of ancient Rome or Greece could tell you with a blush and a flutter of the eyelids, the above assertion is far from being true. Providing that the removal of the testes takes place after puberty, which was most often the case, the eunuch experiences no difficulty at all in achieving an erection. As a result, they were favourite hot-water bottles amongst the ladies of Rome since their attentions didn't carry the risk of pregnancy.

EXECUTIONS UNDER BLOODY MARY WERE EXCESSIVE
It does seem rather unfair to saddle this queen with the title 'Bloody' for, whilst persecution of Protestants undoubtedly took place during her reign, (1553–8) such executions numbered less than 300 which averages out to sixty per year and, for a monarch of that era embarked upon a programme of religious suppression, this would indicate a considerable degree of self-restraint rather than blood-lust.

The trouble with Mary was that she was a miserable old sour-puss and extremely unpopular with all and sundry. Her marriage to Philip II of Spain was repugnant to her subjects and the loss of Calais was blamed on her. In other words, if she hadn't been given this soubriquet she would have ended up with another equally unpleasant one.

EYES CAN BE REMOVED AND REPLACED WITHOUT DAMAGE

This is one of my favourite myths and has been ever since it provoked a furious row in a pub which culminated with the inevitably stupid bets flying left, right and centre. Not only were there people who maintained the above to be routine but, believe it or not, two of those present actually claimed that, after accidents of one type or another, such had been done to them as an out-patient in the local hospital. All of those present who were arguing the case and who reckoned that they had seen this trick done, had had it done to themselves or to a friend, or knew exactly where to exert pressure to make the eyeball pop miraculously out of its socket, really believed what they were saying, and this more than anything else convinced me of the staggering power of myth. If someone wants to believe a load of old rubbish, there is nothing that you can do to alter their opinion.

Without going into the problems presented by the optic nerve and the 40,000,000 odd nerve endings at the back of the eye, all of which would be torn if the eye was pulled as much as a fraction of an inch forwards, there is no way to remove an eye from its socket for the purpose of irrigation or other treatment. If a splinter of material enters the eye but is non-magnetic, you could be in a lot of trouble for it is only with powerful magnets that foreign objects are removed. The human body is not a Leggo kit and an eye can be removed and replaced with about the same degree of success as the brain.

F

'FALL' IS AN AMERICANISM FOR 'AUTUMN'

It may well be far more common in America than here, but Americanism it most certainly is not. 'Fall' is good old Elizabethan English and appears in the works of Drayton, Middleton and Raleigh. The word is but one of many that travelled out to the New World with early settlers who retained such terminology long after it had been abandoned by their native land.

FALLS – MYTHS SURROUNDING

It is probably no longer necessary to state that people who fall from great heights do not die long before they hit the ground, but there are still one or two odd notions attached to falling bodies of the human kind.

The idea is very common that falling people can reach such a high velocity that drawing breath becomes impossible and death ensues from asphyxia. Unless a deliberate and concerted effort is made to maintain an aerodynamic and headlong dive, the human body will not exceed 125 mph, no matter how long it falls for. About 1,900 feet and fourteen seconds are required to achieve this terminal (an unfortunate choice of word perhaps) velocity, so it is fair to say that surviving a fall of around 30,00 feet (and some people have) is no more impressive than walking away from a fall of 2,000 feet. Only the landing site is relevant to survival, and as for people suffocating en route to their sudden stop, people travel faster than 125 mph on motor-bikes every day and survive.

To date, the record holder for the longest drop is a Yugoslav air hostess named Vensa Vulovic who, in 1972, fell 33,330 feet after the mid-air explosion of her

DC9. Despite several months of hospitalisation, she survived and married a man who had nothing to do with aeroplanes.

FARADAY INVENTED THE ELECTRO-MAGNET
Not according to Faraday he didn't! As he always asserted, the discovery was made by William Sturgeon in 1820, he in turn basing his work on the published papers of the Danish physicist Hans Oersted who was the first to establish a link between electricity and magnetism.

'FEMALE' AND 'MALE'
Ultimately derived from Latin where it meant 'the suckling one,' 'female' is not just the word 'male' with a differentiating prefix. Indeed, the current spelling only came into being as a direct result of that very misconception. Originally the word was 'femelle', the second part of the word still alive and well in French where it serves as the pronoun 'she'.

FIFTY POUND NOTES ARE THE HIGHEST DENOMINATION EVER ISSUED
Until 1945 there were loads of £1,000 notes in circulation, and the old yarn 'The Million Pound Note' was not just a flight of fancy. In 1812, the Bank of England raised two such impractical notes and, as recently as 1948, the Treasury issued one of similar denomination.

FIRST ARMOURED MARINE ENGAGEMENT
The two vessels participating in this dubious historical honour are always said to be the USS *Monitor* and the

CSS *Merrimack*, who sat pooping off at each other in Hampton Roads Harbour, Virginia, during the American Civil War.

The only trouble with this is that the Confederacy never had a ship called the *Merrimack*. The USS *Merrimack* had been burnt out and scuttled in the same location earlier in the war. The South raised her and used the remains as the basis for a new ironclad called the CSS *Virginia*. Since the Union won the war, they wrote the history books and constantly referred to the *Virginia* under the name that they had known her by. But if they were going to do that, they should call her the USS *Merrimack*, but that would sound as if they were shooting at themselves which would never do.

The aforementioned ships may have been the first ironclads to engage in anger, but they were not the first *per se*. The French *Glorie* and the British *Warrior* were both in service long before, and *Warrior* was built completely of iron.

FIRST FLUSHING LOOS AND THOMAS CRAPPER

This completely fallacious story still persists having been given a new lease of life by Wallace Reyburn's spoof book *Flushed with Pride – The Story of Thomas Crapper*, published in 1969. Naturally enough, the story maintains that the common vulgarism 'crap' is a contraction, for want of a better word, of the 'inventor's' name. Some people just can't tell when they are being kidded.

'Crap' derives quite straightforwardly from the Middle English 'crappe', which meant residue or rubbish, and the real and true inventor of the first flushing loo in England was an even stranger character than the elusive T. Crapper Esq, for he was none other than Queen Elizabeth I's godson, Sir John Harrington, whom she booted out of the palace for spreading gossip and telling dirty jokes about high ranking dignitaries, including herself. Harrington chose to spend his exile at Kelston near Bath and, keeping his mind in the sewer, he designed, built and installed England's very first flushing loo.

In 1592, Elizabeth, having forgiven her wayward godson, visited him at Kelston. He invited her to pass an opinion on his brainchild which she did by bestowing the high accolade of the 'Royal We' upon Harrington's invention and ordering him to present her with one forthwith.

FISH IS BRAINFOOD

This piece of nonsense originated at the hands of Friedrich Buchner, a nineteenth-century German physician who, having established the presence of phosphorus in the human brain, pronounced that this presence was the medium for rational thought. At about the same time a French chemist called Dumas issued a paper on the high content of phosphorus to be found in fish and, putting two and two together and coming up with eight, a dotty old Swiss naturalist called Jean Louis Agassiz declared that fish was therefore 'brainfood', and the public have been swallowing it ever since.

FLAGS AT HALF-MAST FLY HALFWAY DOWN THE FLAGPOLE

Although the very wording of the above would seem logical, this is not in fact the case. The official description of the term half-mast is that the flag should be lowered until its top corner, that one nearest the flagpole, is at the point where its bottom corner had been. In other words, it should only be lowered by its own depth. It is, of course, true that in the case of a very large flag on a very short pole the flag might well fly literally at half-mast, but this would be pure coincidence.

FLEMING DISCOVERED PENICILLIN
'Fraid not. As far back as 1881, the very year of Fleming's birth, T.H. Huxley, in his publication *Science and Culture*, wrote about 'penicillium', detailing how to produce the stuff and how long it took to grow. The first accurate description of the mould came from Scandinavia in 1911 and Fleming gave it the name 'penicillin' in 1929.

FORT KNOX IS THE WORLD'S LARGEST GOLD DEPOSITORY
Fort Knox certainly has the most charismatic name when it comes to the subject of gold, but at least five times the tonnage can be found lurking in the subterranean vaults of the Federal Reserve Bank in Manhattan.

FREEZE-PLUGS IN CAR ENGINES
There never has been any part of an engine block designed to pop out in the event of a freeze-up and thereby prevent a fracture. The round plugs in the wall of an engine block are there as a result of the manufacturing process and have nothing to do with the ongoing protection of the motor.

Any engine that is water cooled must, by necessity, have double walls separated by a cavity through which the water can flow. During casting this cavity is filled with sand which, after cooling, has to be removed by shaking it out of holes which are subsequently filled with what people like to call freeze-plugs.

FRENCH FOREIGN LEGION AS A HAVEN FOR WANTED CRIMINALS

This famous, or infamous, fighting body has never been a bolt-hole for murderers and cut-throats. Founded in 1831 by Louis Philippe to control the French colonies in Africa, the Legion still permits applicants to assume a *nom de guerre* and to be referred to by such, but his genuine details must be listed for the Legion's records and normal extradition laws apply. As recently as 1984, two men were turned over to English detectives conducting a murder inquiry. Being a Légionnaire has never placed a barrier between a culprit and the law. What serious military body would want its ranks swelled by the kind of human offal that such a convenience would attract.

All applicants are screened by Interpol and the Deuxième Bureau because of this very myth. Only after they have been given the all-clear are they allowed to go ahead and sign their five-year contracts. Personally, I'd rather do ten years in Wormwood Scrubbs than five in the French Foreign Legion, but there it is. During the few days between their application and their acceptance, aspiring Beau Gestes remain 'guests' of the Legion, just in case they are wanted by any police force.

FRENCH FRIES

The word 'French' here describes a cooking method in which the food is cut into strips prior to cooking. Thus, it may be legitimately applied to any vegetable or meat so dealt with. So, the correct response to people who insist on asking you if you mean French fries when you have asked for chips, is 'French fried what?'

Nor are French fried potatoes a French innovation. Potatoes were first Frenched and deep fried by the Belgians and sold from little street kiosks for the customer to take home. These therefore qualify as the first chip shops. From Belgium, the humble chip invaded France, then England, und zen ze verld!

FRENCH GENERALS KISSING SOLDIERS ON PARADE

Although it always looks as if French Staff Officers enjoy a more intimate relationship with their men than is proper, this is not in fact the case. After awarding a medal, or whatever, the senior officer merely touches cheeks with the recipient; he never kisses him, well, not in public at any rate. The gesture is simply a variant of the ancient ritual of bestowing an honour, such as a knighthood. Nowadays this is done with a sword, but the accolade was originally bestowed with the clenched fist. 'Accolade' derives from the Latin *ad collum* – meaning to the neck.

FROSTBITE SHOULD BE TREATED WITH SNOWPACKS

Quite how the ridiculous notion came about that frostbite should be treated by rubbing the damaged areas with snow is unclear. It makes about as much sense as treating burns with a blowtorch. Needless to say, it is a misconception or it wouldn't be included in this book, but it is more than a silly one, it is a potentially lethal one.

In adverse conditions it is extremely unwise to attempt the thawing of frostbite in the field since the most severe tissue damage occurs in the event of refreezing. Nothing should be attempted until the patient can be moved to a location where full and lasting treatment can be given. Before removing the victim from the field, the injured parts should not be packed in snow or rubbed with it; frostbitten tissue should not be rubbed with anything under any circumstances. Nor should the patient be given handwarmers, which is another well-intentioned bad turn often done for sufferers. A slow thaw is infinitely more dangerous than leaving well alone until the proper treatment can be given.

FUNNY BONE
It is not a bone at all but the exposed area of the ulnar nerve. The somewhat unscientific name is the result of a pun on the fact that the bone which runs from the shoulder to the elbow is called the humerus.

G

GALILEO, THE INQUISITION AND THE INVENTION OF THE TELESCOPE
The Inquisition did not harm a hair on Galileo's withered old head, let alone torture him. He was never even arrested but did spend some time under a kind of open detention in his own home.

The most popular myth attached to his heresy trial in respect of his insistence that the earth moved round the sun is that, after recanting, he muttered '*Eppur si muove!*' ('And yet it does move!') under his breath. Why should he risk his life for such an empty, puerile gesture for, had anyone present heard him, he would have been Homo-oxide within the hour – you didn't play games with the Inquisition. And if he did say it and nobody heard him, how did anyone know that he had said it, if you follow me. Naturally enough, the story didn't emerge until over a century after Galileo's death when it was safe to strap him up with any old yarn.

Nor did he invent the telescope. In 1608, Hans Lippershey, an obscure optician of Middleberg, Holland, completed his work on three telescopes. In 1609,

working on Lippershey's designs, Galileo laboured
to make one of his own.

GENDARMES ARE FRENCH POLICEMEN
Although many would bet confidently on the above
assertion, gendarmes are soldiers, not policemen. Their
name meaning simply 'armed people' they were raised as
a military body during the French Revolution; they
come under the direct control of the Minister of Armies,
and are still considered to be military personnel by the
civil authorities. The misconception is quite understandable in England where, to all intents and purposes, we
have but the one police force, whereas in France they
have three. Apart from the Gendarmerie Nationale, who
to be fair do undertake civil duties, there are the
Préfecture de Police, and the Sûreté Nationale.

GIN AND GENEVA
Although the drink that floated the British Empire and,
had she been around, would have made Britannia waive
all the rules, was once known as geneva, that Swiss city
has no connection with it. Such flavour as there is in gin
is there by virtue of the juniper berry, juniper once being
known as *genévre* in Old French.

GLOW-WORMS
But one of the many misnomers in the animal world,
these creatures are actually beetles. To be precise, they
are the wingless lava-like females of the lampyrid beetle
whose sixth and seventh abdominal segments emit a
coloured glow. It's much easier to call the damn things
glow-worms, isn't it.

'GOD REST YOU MERRY, GENTLEMEN'

Every year, thousands of carol singers chant this line with completely the wrong emphasis, believing that the line should read 'God rest you, merry Gentlemen'. When the line was written, 'merry' didn't have the connotations of gaiety and frivolity that it does today; the comma should always come after the word 'merry' and the line means 'May God grant you peace, Gentlemen', and not 'May God grant you happy chappies rest'. In earlier times, 'merry' meant pleasing, pleasant or suitable.

'GOD TEMPERS THE WIND TO THE SHORN LAMB'

Yet another quote with a distinctly biblical ring to it, but which is really of far more recent and secular origins. The line was popularised by Laurence Sterne's *A Sentimental Journey*, but the original use seems to lie with Henri Estienne, the French scholar and publisher.

GOLF ORIGINATED IN SCOTLAND

It is more than possible that this myth grew up in America as a result of the game having been introduced into that country in 1888 by John Reid and his entourage of golf-crazed fellow Scots. They were known collectively as the Apple Tree Gang because they constructed a six-hole golf course in an apple orchard in Yonkers. It may well be true that golf has had a long history in Scotland, but the game did not develop there.

The word seems to stem from the Dutch *kolf*, which was a club used in the ancient and similar Dutch game of *kolven*. In addition to this, Scotland used to import her golf balls from Holland, so we could be looking at a Dutch game. Having said all that, the Scots certainly took to the game like ducks to water and, as a sport, it first rivalled and then superseded archery. Since the latter was infinitely more useful during times of trouble and strife, golf was actually outlawed under pain of death in Scotland, in March 1457.

GOOSEBERRY FOOL
Despite the light and woolly consistency of gooseberry fool, stupidity does not enter the question. The dish is prepared by mashing up the fruit and forcing the resultant mush through a sieve. 'Fool' is but a corruption of *foule*, the French term for pressing or crushing.

GOTHIC ARCHITECTURE
The Goths had no architectural skills whatsoever. They were far more interested in razing buildings than raising them. The designation was coined during the Renaissance by traditionalist artists and architects who saw the style as a travesty and responsible for the diminishing interest in the classical Graeco-Roman style so dear to their hearts. Since it had been the Goths who had invaded the Roman Empire and actually got as far as sacking Rome itself, their name was used.

GOUT
The notion that there is a link between rich living (especially the excessive consumption of port) and gout originated in the eighteenth century when cartoonists showed overweight and ageing squires riddled with gout and sitting at tables laden with food and wine. To be fair, this image was a pretty accurate one, in that the average British aristo was something of a Christmas pudding in that he was incredibly thick, disgustingly rich, and normally so full of brandy that he would catch fire if you put a match to him. Be this as it may, their

lifestyle wasn't responsible for the gout that struck at rich and poor alike, as indeed it still does today.

Port was then a fairly new drink in England and therefore far too expensive for the common herd who eagerly seized upon it as the cause of the gout that seemed so prevalent among the drink-sodden heirs and Graces. The truth of the matter is that the poor suffered equally from the condition but, not being able to afford a doctor, never knew what was ailing them. To this day, the cause of the condition remains unknown and it is just as likely to strike down a teetotal Trappist monk with a penchant for marathon running as it is anyone.

GRASP THE NETTLE FIRMLY

This may work well in the realm of metaphor, but anyone who really believes that a violently grasped nettle has neither the time nor the capacity to inflict injury is strongly advised to buy a large tube of soothing lotion before conducting any field trials.

GRASSHOPPERS RUB THEIR BACK LEGS TOGETHER

They'd most likely fall over if they tried this. Grasshoppers stridulate, as the action is known, by grating their wings together. Sometimes the noise is produced by rubbing their wings against their legs – but never by employing both legs.

THE GREAT FIRE OF LONDON CLAIMED THOUSANDS OF LIVES

Although commonly held to be the purgative saviour that stamped out the plague, the Great Fire of London did no such thing. It certainly laid waste the greater part of the city, razing 90 churches and 13,200 dwellings, but the rat-infested slums that were the plague's stronghold were almost completely untouched. Besides, the plague died out in all the other major centres without such a holocaust.

In reality the fire death-toll was incredibly small, accounting for only four lives. Had the plague not already sated its appetite on the population of London, the figure would undoubtedly have been significantly higher. Perhaps this is easier to understand with the knowledge that the population of London would have been a scant 40,000 when the fire broke out. Of a total estimated population of 460,000, well over two-thirds had fled the city generously taking the sickness to parts of the countryside that might otherwise have missed out on all the fun. Of those that remained, the plague took anything up to approximately 100,000 which meant that when the fire broke out on 2 September 1666 it could only rage impotently through a ghost-town.

Just in case you are interested, the famous four are as follows. Alice, a simpleton girl in the employ of the Farynor family at whose baking premises the fire started; an unknown old woman who, with a misplaced trust in the Lord wisely unshared by those she besought to follow her, sought refuge in the old St Paul's shortly before it exploded in a ball of fire; an old man, last seen returning to his burning house to retrieve some bedding; and Paul Lowell, a watchmaker of Shoe Lane who, dismissing the fire as nothing out of the ordinary and the dangers as exaggerated, announced his intention to stay in his house until it fell on top of him. Of course, it did. Some estimates place the death toll at the dizzy heights of six, but this includes two drunks who fell into the river and drowned when running from a burning building, so they don't really count.

GREEK AND ROMAN SCULPTURE WAS PLAIN AND UNCOLOURED

That is certainly the way that all museums choose to exhibit their collections, but when the statues graced Athens or Rome they were not only fully painted but also fully clothed. With modern techniques, it is quite possible to determine the original colour schemes but, since they sound as if the overall impression would have had about as much taste as British Rail coffee, perhaps the misconception is altogether more acceptable.

GREEN VEGETABLES ARE THE BEST SOURCE OF IRON

The human body is extremely inefficient at extracting iron from vegetables, it being incapable of removing in excess of 10 per cent of the total content. Sometimes that figure can drop to 2 per cent. Red meats are actually the best source of iron since the presence of amino acids means that the absorption rate can shoot up to about 30 per cent of the gross which, in the case of, for example, liver, is considerably higher than any vegetable to begin with.

GREYHOUNDS IN THE BIBLE

People often nominate the greyhound as the oldest known breed because it is mentioned in the Bible. This may be true, but the dog mentioned in the Good Book won't have been that which is called a greyhound today. The greyhound classification includes the saluki which will have been the dog of biblical lands and times. This extremely fleet and elegant hound is without question the oldest of all breeds, carvings of it having been found in the East and dated to c.7000 BC. The dog would appear to have been named after the ancient Arab city of Saluq.

Funnily enough, even though the typical greyhound is grey in colour, this has nothing to do with the term. The English language built the word on the Icelandic *greybaka* which meant bitch, a term once applied willy-nilly to any dog irrespective of its sex.

GUNSLINGERS PUT NOTCHES IN THEIR GUNS
No one engaged in this sort of pointless boast since they would have had good cause to regret it the first time they were called upon to fire more than a couple of rounds. The kick from a heavy .45 was severe and after protracted firing the holder was only too painfully aware of this fact. If in addition the pistol grip had been serrated with sharp V-shaped notches, the firer would soon find himself in need of a little first aid to his gun hand.

It seems that the myth was started accidentally by Bat Masterson who retired to New York to die with his boots off. He was constantly being pestered by a local gun collector for one of his frontier day Colts and, just to shut the man up, Masterson says that he popped into some gun shop or other, bought an old Colt and, for sheer devilment, cut twenty-two notches in the handle before selling it to the ecstatic collector at an immoral profit. This was just the sort of thing that the Easterners loved to believe about their cowboy heroes and they imagined that everybody did it.

H

HAIR AND NAILS CONTINUE TO GROW AFTER DEATH

Not so! They stop just like everything else. A freshly shaved corpse may, at some time after death, appear to have grown stubble, but this is due to tissue shrinkage rather than beard growth.

Several historical personages have been said to have turned grey overnight from shock or grief, even people today claim to know someone who has experienced a similar traumatic change. Hair can only grow grey from the roots and existing hair, having already been coloured, will retain its pigmentation until dyed or pulled out. Such an apparent phenomenon in history could only have been caused by the abandonment of a wig for effect.

HANDEL – HIS 'MESSIAH' AND HIS 'WATER MUSIC'

There are a couple of misconceptions attached to these two most popular works of this composer. 'Messiah', not 'The Messiah' as is generally seen, was not first performed by Royal Command at Covent Garden but in the unlikely venue of a music hall in Fishamble Street, Dublin, on 13 April 1742. The purpose of the concert was to raise money to save a number of debtors from the local debtors prison. It was almost a year before the King heard the piece, and despite its now indissoluble links with Christmas it was not written with that festival in mind.

Next we have the story that in an attempt to get back into George II's good books, Handel composed 'Water Music' and, knowing the King was to take a river trip, hired a boat and an orchestra to float alongside the royal party playing the new piece. It makes as nice a story as it is widely accepted, but there never was any trouble between the two that needed patching up.

HAREMS
Forgetting the image that Hollywood has tried to hammer into the minds of Westerners, a Moslem harem is not a place filled with veiled voluptuaries with nothing better to do than satisfy the sexual cravings of some lecherous potentate. In Arabic the word is *harim* and means 'forbidden'; it describes that part of a residence set apart for the female members of the household. Apart from the wife or wives, the area is used by female servants and relatives alike, so harems are far from the private brothels of cinematic fantasy.

HARI KIRI
The Japanese do not use the above term at all; they call the ritual 'seppuku', which is rarely the gory act of Western imagination. Almost invariably the suicide's 'best man' was in attendance, equipped with a freshly sharpened sword. Sometimes the suicide's head was whipped off the instant the knife entered the abdomen; other times as soon as he picked up the ceremonial knife – that gesture of intent being sufficient to satisfy the senior for whose benefit the silly ritual was taking place. 'Seppuku' is now illegal in Japan.

HEAT RISES
It does not. The property of heat behaves in a very similar manner to fluids in that it attempts to disperse itself equally throughout its environment. Heat flows from areas of high temperature to areas of low, be it

required to travel up, down or sideways. It is heated air and water that rise, having become lighter. If you doubt this, hold an iron bar in one hand, play a blow-torch at the top, and see how long you can hold on to the bar.

HEDGEHOGS – MYTHS SURROUNDING

Hedgehogs do not collect fallen fruit by rolling over, impaling it on their spines before scurrying off to their lairs with the booty. Why should they? Fruit is of almost negligible interest to the animal, besides, it hibernates during the winter months and stores no food at all, and when awake, it always dines out.

Next we have the endearing image of armies of hedgehogs trotting into the fields at dawn to milk sleeping cows. Hedgehogs are possessed of some pretty sharp teeth and if they latched on to an udder its owner would get up very rapidly. Hedgehogs have been seen lapping up milk leaked from overfull cows' udders, but this is hardly the same thing.

It is perhaps inevitable that the sexual performance of a creature of such anatomical design should become the subject of jokes, speculation and misinformation. If hedgehogs encountered all the problems in mating that humans imagine, then the poor little things would have died out years ago. The female merely flattens her spines and they proceed as normal, normal for hedgehogs, that is. Nor is pain caused or damage done to the mother by the spines of the young during birth for the simple reason that the young don't have any. At birth, the skin boasts only little pimples that are the spine-sites. A couple of hours after delivery, soft, white 'milk-spines' appear, the adult ones come later.

Lastly, hedgehogs don't 'need' the fleas that infest them; this is the other edge of the sword that is their armour. It is impossible for the animal to rid itself of its unwelcome guests. Whilst it is perfectly true that the creature seems to live quite happily with its parasites, it would doubtless live a great deal happier without them.

HENS NEED A COCK TO LAY
Widespread is the notion that, without the romantic attentions of a cock, hens will not lay eggs. Left to their own devices hens will lay quite happily; the eggs may be infertile but since they are destined for the frying pan this is irrelevant.

'HERE WE GO GATHERING NUTS IN MAY'
Patently a nonsense since there are no nuts that fall ready for collection in the month of May. The above children's chant is actually a corruption of 'Here we go gathering knots of may', as in the collection of bunches of May flowers for the May Day celebrations.

HIGH BUILDINGS SWAY IN THE WIND
Firmly entrenched in the popular imagination of virtually every nation is the idea that the sky-scraping monstrosities of cities like New York sway several feet in the wind. It's a great pity that they don't, because if they did they'd fall down. The famous Empire State building is often said to sway as much as 12 feet or more, but in reality it only moves an absolute maximum of 2 inches from the vertical, and this is an ongoing shift, nothing to do with the wind. This works out to something less than .0016 of an inch per foot rise of the building, which is hardly flapping about in the breeze.

HITLER – MYTHS SURROUNDING
Hitler's name was Hitler, it was not Schicklegruber. Hitler was the son of Alois Hitler, a shoemaker turned

customs officer, and his third wife Karla Poelzl, a girl twenty-three years his junior who had been a maid in his first wife's house. Alois had been born out of wedlock to Maria Anna Schicklegruber and Johann Huettler, that couple not marrying until their son was 5. Alois did not legally hold his father's name, variously spelt Huettler, Hitler and Hiedler, until he was 35. By the time young Adolph appeared the family name was definitely and legally Hitler. The 'Schicklegruber' tag was revived by his political opponents in the 1930s and eagerly seized on by the Allied propaganda machine to ridicule him.

Hitler never worked as a house-painter but, like Churchill, was not a bad hand with brush and canvas. In fact, there are some who say that had he persisted he probably would have been accepted by the Berlin Academy and we could have missed out on the Second World War.

Without doubt, the best loved of all the Hitler myths is that he ended up absolutely gaga with syphillis. That the man was mad as a hatter is probably beyond dispute, but it doesn't seem that he was clinically insane. Heavily into astrology and other sorts of hokum, it was perhaps a foregone conclusion that Hitler should appoint a charlatan quack as his personal physician; it was pure coincidence that Theo Morell was also Berlin's most fashionable pox-doctor.

HOI POLLOI

Perhaps due to its similarity to 'hoity-toity', this expression is all too often used to describe the so-called upper classes whereas, 'hoi polloi' being Greek for 'the many', the expression in fact describes the common herd.

Purists do tend to get a little excited when the phrase appears as 'the hoi polloi' since 'hoi' already means 'the' but if people like Byron and Dryden got away with it, why can't we?

HOMER WROTE THE ILLIAD

There is significant doubt whether there ever was any such person as Homer. As early as the Hellenistic period (356–23 BC) scholars were expressing severe doubt about the authenticity of the character, maintaining instead the work attributed to Homer to be the endeavours of many writers which had been knocked into shape by a group of scholars or one very industrious individual. This is extremely possible since the details of Homer's life are as sketchy and contradictory as those of the equally non-existent Aesop, and tradition places him in more places at one time than Lord Lucan.

HOMING PIGEONS AND THEIR 'NATURAL' INSTINCT

If you took such a bird from its loft and released it for the first time a few miles away, it would never return except by sheer fluke. There is no natural, built-in homing instinct, the birds have to be trained beginning with distances measured in feet and within direct sight of 'home'. This must be done from all directions before distances can be extended to be measured in miles. Some say the birds have a high memory factor and that they progress along a line of known landmarks, yet the brids fly through the night. Other theories are based on ideas of solar or lunar navigation, but the truth is that only the pigeons know how they do it.

'HOW', 'PALEFACE' AND ALL THAT JAZZ

Although a few Indian languages did include the word *hao* in their vocabularies, and that word did hold a literal meaning of 'Hello', in general speech it was only used as an expletive indicating surprise or anger; it was never employed as a greeting. The confusion over the word's application seems to have been caused by self-appointed 'Indian experts' acting as consultants to the movie business when they did in fact hold no more than a 'hello, goodbye, thank you' knowledge of the languages in question. The same 'specialists' produced the idea that, when attacking a waggon train or whatever, the Indian obligingly rode round and round in circles until he got dizzy or shot, and that Indians would never attack in the dark in case they got killed and their spirit couldn't find its way to the Happy Hunting Ground.

As for those other stock expressions of the downmarket Western, 'Paleface', 'on the warpath', 'warpaint', and the unforgettable 'Whiteman speaks with forked tongue', these were all invented by James Fenimore Cooper for use in his books and never graced the lips of a real, live Indian.

I

'I REGRET THAT I ONLY HAVE BUT ONE LIFE TO LOSE FOR MY COUNTRY'

Fine and stirring words said to be the Parthian shot delivered by Nathan Hale to his British executioners who were about to string him up for spying, he having been betrayed by his own brother. According to statements made by people present at Hale's leap into the unknown, he said no such thing. Such sentiments as his supposed last words had been employed by several characters, both fictional and real, long before Hale's death. Hungry for heroes, the American Revolution just went ahead and pinned the quote to Hale's corpse and said nothing about the fact that he had been turned over to the British by his own family. What Hale actually said on the gallows was: 'It is the duty of every good officer to obey any orders given him by his Commander-in-Chief.'

ICELAND IS A COLD COUNTRY

Despite its name and its abutting the Arctic Circle, Iceland is not a frozen and forbidding wasteland. It is not even a particularly cold place either. It catches warmth from the Gulf Stream, a spur of which encircles it and there are numerous underground hot springs. Throughout the year there is not much more than a 10° C variance in temperature between England and Iceland. Reykyavik, the capital, has almost identical weather patterns to those experienced in New York.

IF THE COWS ARE LYING DOWN IT IS GOING TO RAIN

Although a total myth, this old wives' tale is probably just as good a guide to imminent weather patterns as the usual calibre of forecast issued by the Met. Office. Basically, if the cows are lying down, it means that they're tired.

IHS

It is wholly incorrect to print the above as I.H.S., that being the customary form which gives credence to the myth that the letters represent Iesus Hominum Salvator, (Jesus, Saviour of Men) or In Hac Salus, (Safety in this [the cross]) or In Hoc Signo (In this sign [you will conquer]). IHS is nothing more than the abbreviated form of the Greek equivalent of the name Jesus, which is Iesous, IHS being but the first two and last letters. It is obvious that there is a double misconception here; the 'H' is not an 'H' at all but the long Greek 'E' which just happens to be represented by the symbol 'H'. This was mistaken by those people familiar with the Latin culture, but ignorant of the Greek, as being the letter 'H' as in 'Harry'. Because of this, IES might be better, but either way, I.H.S. makes no more sense than does putting J.I.M. instead of 'James'.

'ILK' AND ITS USAGE

'Ilk' invariably appears in the expression 'of that ilk' and is commonly heard in the sense of 'same', 'similar', or 'approximately the same'. Even though 'ilk' ultimately derives from an Old English word that meant 'same', it means nothing of the kind. The expression is only properly used when talking about someone who comes from a noble estate that bears his name, e.g. Lord Davenport of the Davenport Estate, who may be called 'Davenport of that ilk'.

THE IMMACULATE CONCEPTION REFERS TO JESUS BEING BORN OF A VIRGIN

It does not refer to the birth of Christ at all but to that of the Virgin Mary. The dogma is to the effect that Mary was free of the taint of the strange idea of 'original sin' from the moment she was conceived in her mother's womb. Not defined as being 'of faith' until 8 December 1854, it was a sort of back-dated honour to clear up any awkward questions about Mary being cursed with original sin, just like all the rest of us. You see, the concept of original sin held that it was inescapably passed from generation to generation like some hereditary disease, and if Mary had it, and Christ was born of her in human form . . . well, you can see where that could lead; they had to do something, didn't they?

INDIAN RESTAURANTS AND THE 'DOG IN THE FRIDGE' SYNDROME

Why is it always an alsatian? Why do these callous caterers always go out hunting this one type of dog? Is it that alsatians make more worthy opponents for a deadly game of 'Hide and Sikh' in the dark backstreets? Or is it that Mongrel Madras simply doesn't present the same culinary challenge? Everybody knows that this unsportsman-like behaviour is rife! Everybody has heard of at least one restaurant where the grizzly evidence was discovered in the fridge by shocked Health Inspectors! So why has there never been a single such case prosecuted or documented?

IRAN IS THE MODERN NAME OF PERSIA

Iranians have been calling the country Iran for centuries, only foreigners called it Persia. It was the Greeks who first started calling the place Persia because they were engaged in trade with merchants from the province of Pars, and the name simply spread to embrace the whole country.

IRISH COFFEE ORIGINATED IN IRELAND

As a moment's thought will prove, such a concoction could never have been dreamed up in Ireland where it's hard enough to get them to put water in your whisky, let alone coffee, cream and sugar. It was developed for use in Ireland, but not by the Irish themselves.

The pioneering days of American aviation were pretty spartan. The airlines could, through no fault of their own, offer little in the way of basic comforts like heating and pressurised cabins, and the seaplanes that landed at Foynes in Ireland tended to disgorge some pretty tired, cold and irritable people. The dieticians were consulted as to the best pick-me-up to pour into them and the result was Irish coffee.

IT IS EASIER FOR A CAMEL TO GO THROUGH THE EYE OF A NEEDLE, ETC.

Although the meaning of the above is abundantly clear it is, you will admit, a rather odd choice of comparisons. When translating from Greek, confusion arose due to the similarity between *kamelos* meaning a camel, and *kamilos* meaning a rope, which does, after all, make a lot more sense.

'IT IS MORE BLESSED TO GIVE THAN TO RECEIVE'

Although quite in keeping with the ethos of Jesus's teachings, he never said any such thing during the so-called Sermon on the Mount. It is Paul who issues this statement.

IT IS THE INALIENABLE RIGHT OF EVERY AMERICAN TO KEEP AND BEAR ARMS

The inalienable right of every man-jack in America to go around armed to the teeth is not written into the Constitution. Americans are very fond of stating this to be the case, but there again, they do happen to be inordinately fond of waving guns around and shooting each other. Article Two of the Constitution states that 'A well regulated militia, being necessary to the security of a free State, the right of the people to bear Arms, shall not be infringed'. In other words, anyone who is not a member of a recognised militia unit does not have an inviolate right to carry a gun. Any American government could implement wide-ranging gun restrictions, but that would be political suicide so, just as successive British governments continue to permit the self-depletion of the population with alcohol, tobacco and cars that do well over the legal limit of 70 mph, American administrations prefer to permit their voters the privilege of blowing holes in each other.

IT WAS ILLEGAL TO DRINK IN AMERICA
DURING THE PROHIBITION ERA
Old gangster films always show the customers in a
speakeasy being rounded up and charged, but it was
perfectly legal to drink alcohol throughout the entire
Prohibition farce. To avoid the embarrassment of having
to arrest virtually the entire administration from the
President down, the Volsted Act made it illegal to
manufacture, transport or traffic in alcohol, but anyone
found drinking the stuff was in the clear.

IT TAKES FORTY GALLONS OF WATER TO
PRODUCE ONE PINT OF BEER
This ridiculous myth was started by a public misinformation leaflet littered about by the National Water
Council during the so-called 'drought' of 1976. Despite
the fact that an immediate outcry of derision from the
brewers forced the Council to retract the statement and
admit a figure of five pints to be more accurate, the
damage was already done. The same hysterical hand-out
shrilled that it took a staggering 44,000 gallons of water
to manufacture one car tyre. After the tyre manufacturers sent the Council a rather pointed letter, the figure
was marginally adjusted to 15 gallons.

IVAN THE TERRIBLE WAS TERRIBLE
By today's standards he was probably a touch on the
brutal side, but so were all rulers or they didn't hold on
to the job for long, and their retirement period was
rarely longer than a few seconds. All this aside, we have
our current image of the man due to poor translation of
his epithet, Ivan Grozny, meaning Ivan the Awful, in the
sense of awe-inspiring – once the term's only meaning.
With the complete turnabout in the meaning of 'awful',
we have ended up with Ivan the Terrible.

J

JACK IS THE PET FORM OF JOHN

It may well be employed as such by all and sundry, but that doesn't make it right. Jack is actually short for James. James started out in Hebrew as Jacob and held a meaning of 'one who takes another by the heel', i.e. someone who trips up another, a supplanter, in other words. The name entered Latin as Jacobus before altering to Jacomus. From there it infiltrated French in the form of Jaques, but that is the French James, not Jack or John. It must also be remembered that the followers of the exiled James Stuart were called Jacobites. Johnny is the pet form of John.

1 JANUARY 2000 WILL BE THE FIRST DAY OF THE TWENTY-FIRST CENTURY

Without doubt, this day is going to see some pretty wild celebrations and even more flowery lies of better things to come from our noble leaders, but all that aside, 1 January 2000 will not be the first day of the new millennium; that honour goes to 1 January 2001. From 1 January in the year 1 to 1 January in the year 100 is only ninety-nine years, and so on through the centuries.

'THE JAZZ SINGER' WAS THE FIRST TALKING MOVING PICTURE

Although a smash hit on both sides of the Atlantic, 'The Jazz Singer' of 1927 does not qualify since the sound was produced by nothing more sophisticated than the synchronised playing of gramophone records, and there were only 354 spoken words in the whole film. This system of linking sound to vision was hardly new, people had been producing 'talkies' like that since the Paris Exposition of 1900, and the first sound-on-film process was patented in 1906. The first sound-on-film, all talking feature film was 'In Old Arizona', which was released on 25 December 1928.

JENNER CONDUCTED THE FIRST VACCINATIONS AND INTRODUCED INNOCULATION INTO ENGLAND

The first reliable report of a successful vaccination came in 1771 when Robert Fooks, a butcher of Bridport, Dorset, was so treated before unsuccessful attempts by Mr Downe, a local surgeon, to infect him with small-pox. Even then, the fact that those who had contracted cowpox tended not to pick up smallpox was nothing new to country folk who had been vaccinating each other for years, they just didn't happen to call it such. Although there are no documented cases before Mr Downe tried to kill his butcher, it is widely accepted that in certain rural areas it was a common practice. Edward Jenner did not conduct his first vaccination until 14 May 1796.

Innoculation is even older in practice, the Welsh are known to have been at it as early as the end of the sixteenth century. The person responsible for its intro-duction into England was Lady Mary Wortley Montagu, wife of the British Ambassador to the Otterman Court. She permitted the innoculation of her son whilst in Turkey and campaigned relentlessly for the widespread adoption of the practice upon her return to England in 1717. George I's daughter-in-law was the first significant convert who, after taking the very wise precaution of conducting a few experiments on children from a nearby poor house, innoculated her two daughters. Innocula-tion flourished as a practice until banned in 1840 in favour of the altogether safer precaution of vaccination. Jenner wasn't even born until 1749.

JESUS THE CHRIST AND THE CRUCIFIXION

There is no biblical evidence to support the belief that Jesus's feet were nailed to the cross. Nowhere is there mention of nail wounds in the feet nor any mention of the feet being nailed to the cross in any of the accounts of the crucifixion.

There were several minor variations in crucifixion methods, but the feet were more often than not tied to the cross, indeed, many crosses had a small projection for that very purpose. It is only in John that nail wounds are mentioned at all and then only in the hands, but even this is extremely doubtful since victims who were nailed up were afixed through the wrists; a nail would tear straight through the human hand under the condemned person's weight.

In the gospel attributed to Luke, Jesus appears to the disciples after the resurrection and says: 'Behold my hands and my feet, that it is I myself, handle me and see, for a spirit hath not flesh and bones, as ye see me have.' No mention of nail wounds at all! It must be remembered that, with the obvious exception of the head, the current dress concealed all but the hands and feet. Jesus was not trying to identify himself to them by showing wounds, somewhat unnecessary as they would surely know him well enough by his face, rather he was trying to convince them of his physical tangibility. Most significant of all is that Doubting Thomas refuses to go along with the idea that the figure is Christ risen unless he can touch the nail wounds in the hands (this part of the gospel was evidently written by someone who was not there at the time) and the spear thrust in the side. Had there been any nail wounds in the feet, Thomas would have wanted to touch those as well.

Also it is inconceivable that Jesus would have been made to carry the entire cross to the execution ground; he would have been physically incapable of doing so. More often than not, it was only the cross-member that the victim carried after he had been lashed to it. If the offender had been flogged first, he was incapable of even this and, under pain of death for refusal, an able bodied man was drawn from the crowd to bear the burden. In Jesus's case, the man was a Cyrenian named Simon.

As for the shape of the cross, it wouldn't have been the standard Latin cross as seen in churches throughout the world, but the Tau, or T-shaped cross. On the subject of the cross itself, there are said to be enough 'genuine' pieces around today to make up several crosses, which is all well and good, but no one would have been allowed to stroll up and hack lumps out of Roman Army Property, nor would the crosses have been left unattended after the removal of the bodies. With the dearth of stout trees in the Holy Land (olive trees are no use for lumber), timber of any description was extremely scarce and all crosses would have been returned to stores before the execution squad could sign off. The same would go for any unused nails as well; all would have to be accounted for.

As to the actual cause of death on the cross, this is popularly imagined to be shock, blood loss, or sunstroke/hunger/thirst, or a combination thereof, but all are a long way wide of the mark. The Romans intended death to be a long time coming. Crucifixion was not only intended to serve as a grim execution method, but also as a salutary warning to all and sundry that retribution from Rome was swift, ruthless and highly unpleasant. A competent execution officer could keep a man alive on the cross for over three days. Nails, as already stated, were not only expensive but wholly unnecessary to the procedure and most people were simply tied hand and foot to the cross. After hanging by

81

the arms for a short time, violent cramps beset the chest making breathing extremely difficult and painful as a result of pressure thus exerted on the diaphragm. This can only be alleviated by the victim taking the weight on his legs, then back to his arms again, and so forth until, too tired or dispirited to continue the procedure, he slumps and dies of asphyxia. That's right, suffocation is what kills you on the cross. Anyone left hanging by the arms, no matter what the method of fixing, will soon die.

JESUS THE CHRIST WAS BORN IN A STABLE IN BETHLEHEM ON 25 DECEMBER 1 BC

The use of the word 'the' in this heading and that of the preceding entry is quite deliberate. The man's name was not, at the risk of sounding flippant, Mr J. Christ, although that is most often the implication. His name was Jesus of Nazareth, or, if you want to be really fussy, Jesus gen Nazareth. 'Christ' was a title bestowed upon him by his followers who used the Greek *Kristos* meaning 'Anointed One', so, just as people say Jesus, the Messiah, they should also say Jesus, the Christ.

There is not a single, reliable biblical source to back up any of the assertions made in the heading; indeed, the whole concept and popular image of the birth of Jesus is one of pure Western invention and fantasy. It is only in the now accepted versions of the gospels attributed to Matthew and Luke that we get any mention of the time, place and manner of the event – Mark and John avoid the issue completely, which is significant in itself. Almost universally recognised as having been written around a century after the events that they describe, and clumsily attached to the front of the gospels concerned, the two conflicting accounts of the Nativity are not only highly contradictory, but are at best extremely shaky and full of holes, and at the worst pure fabrication. This latter does seem to be the most likely of the two possibilities. Jesus is known to have grown up in Nazareth and there is no earthly reason why he shouldn't have been born there as well. There were, however, unearthly reasons for the birth to be moved to Bethlehem and, because the old prophecies foretold that the Messiah would be born in Bethlehem, whoever it was that revamped Matthew and Luke turned history on its head to contrive the birth to have taken place in Bethlehem and thus corroborate and reaffirm Jesus's credibility as the Christ.

According to Matthew, Jesus's parents were resident in Bethlehem in a house at the time of the delivery and, in so far as the circumstances and physical surroundings are concerned, he reports nothing unusual. Matthew (we shall call him that for the sake of argument and extend the same privilege to Luke) now has a problem in that he has to get the family back to Nazareth where they really belong. This he achieves, via Egypt, by the invention of the so-called slaughter of the innocents by Herod, and by having Joseph forewarned of the grizzly event by a heaven-sent dream. Matthew would appear to be the only person who considered this incredible act of wholesale infanticide worthy of mention. It is not mentioned anywhere else in the Bible and there is not a scrap of corroborative historical evidence to back it up. In short, it simply didn't happen. Matthew most likely got the idea from the story of the Pharoah who put all the Hebrew first-born to the sword.

Luke is even more inventive in his attempt to place the birth in the desired place. He tells us that Joseph and Mary lived in Nazareth but that, while Mary was pregnant, they had to go to Bethlehem to be counted in the Roman census being organised by Cyrenius. Everyone, Luke tells us, had to return to the city of his lineage to be counted. Joseph was of the House of David; Bethlehem was the City of David – ergo, Joseph and Mary must go to Bethlehem. Now, this may well sound all very plausible, but if there is one thing known about Roman census-taking methods it was that everyone stayed put, kept travelling to a minimum and waited for the officials to get round to them. Can you imagine the chaos caused by half the country suddenly going walkabout the length and breadth of the nation, not to mention whole family groups having to abandon their farms, crops, homes and livestock for weeks on end while they trekked off to some distant city. Nazareth to Bethlehem, for example, is some eighty-odd miles. So, did they live in Nazareth and go to Bethlehem, or did they live in Bethlehem and escape to Nazareth. It can't be both. Most strikingly of all, the Cyrenius census is known to have taken place in the year AD 6 and Herod to have died in 4 BC. To put it bluntly, both are lying, and the most disturbing thing about that is the question as to why they should feel the need to do so in the first place. Why not just ignore the whole question as did the other two gospels.

It is, to say the least, extraordinary that when it comes to the most talked-about and significant figure in Western culture, nobody knows where he was born, when he was born, or even when he died. This has not, however, stopped the speculation. Various astronomers through the ages have tried to pinpoint the year by linking it to the occurrence of known celestial phenomena – not least of all Halley's comet. Such speculation is all very well, but such an approach to the question presupposes the existence of the so-called Star of Bethlehem, and we only have Matthew's very shaky word for that. At the end of the day, no one knows when the birth took place. The first mention of Christmas being celebrated on the now traditional date appears in the Philocalian Calendar of the year 336. It was over a century later, in 440, when the Church finally fixed the date for Christmas. There was no Christian motivation for the choice of 25 December, rather the opposite since they pitched the ceremony to coincide with two of the most significant pagan ceremonies, the Yule of Northern Europe, and the Roman Dies Natalis Invicti Solis (Birthday of the Unconquered Sun). The early Church always found it easier to adulterate and adopt, or simply blend in with existing pagan practice rather than attempt to eradicate it.

Probably fixed for all time is the image of Jesus being born in a stable, warm and snug with the animals while the snow lay deep outside – in the Middle East? Again, this is all Western invention and there is not a scrap of biblical foundation. The Luke account of events simply states that whilst in Bethlehem 'the days were accomplished that she should be delivered'. This is hardly the last-minute dash across the desert that looms so large in the popular imagination. The first Greek translation of Luke speaks of the birth taking place in a *katalemma* – that term applying to any temporary shelter or cave. Early Christian tradition certainly places the birth in a cave, and it was over a cave that Constantine built the Bethlehem Church of the Nativity. Caves, it must be remembered, would have been highly desirable places to use for shelter given the climate in that they are always cool and would therefore have been ideal for the strenuous business of labour. Luke also tells us that the Last Supper took place in a *katalemma*, yet no one has so far seriously suggested that Jesus and the disciples got together in a stable for a meal. Similar licence has been taken with the word *thaten* in that most Bibles show it as 'manger'. When used in conjunction with a baby, *thaten* means only 'crib' and nothing else.

Quite understandably, the majority of people have the image of Jesus as an only child, whereas he actually had four brothers – James, Joses, Simeon and Jude, and two sisters, names unknown. This certainly puts quite a heavy strain on the concept of the ever-virgin Mary. Nor

85

was Jesus a carpenter in the way that we understand the term. In his time, the word meant something more akin to a general builder.

JET ENGINES PUSH THE 'PLANE ALONG
If it were true that the thrust of a jet engine somehow pushed against the surrounding atmosphere then they would never work in space; yet they do so even more efficiently. The more rarefied the atmosphere, the better they function because they do so on the principle of action and reaction. Because there is a high velocity exhaust behind the 'plane it has no option but to move in the opposite direction. If you strapped on roller skates and tossed a couple of bricks to your rear, you would be moved forward by the same principles that drive the most advanced jets.

JOAN OF ARC WAS SO NAMED AND WAS FRENCH
Neither is true. She was born at Domremy in Lorraine in 1442, that being an independent duchy which did not fall to France until 1766. Her father is recorded as having told her that he would strangle her with his own two hands if she went into France, so it certainly doesn't sound as if he thought of himself as a Frenchman. The family name was Darc, and not d'Arc, as the English have twisted it over the years, and her family called her Jhennette. Finally, she wasn't the young girl of simple peasant stock that she is always portrayed; her father was an extremely successful farmer and was Domremy's leading citizen.

Little is heard of her after her death, until Napoleon resurrected her as some kind of cult figure. Around the turn of this century (she wasn't even canonised until 1920 and some say the Vatican were reluctant to do so even then), there were those who thought that Boney had gone just a little too far and dipped his paint-brush deep into the paint-pot of tradition to portray the figure he wanted as the embodiment of the Gallic spirit; a sort of St Georgina, if you like. Many consider her involvement and importance in the Hundred Years War to be grossly exaggerated, if not partly fiction to one degree or another. There are examples of writings that refer to her as being nothing more than 'one of many maids who followed the Army as a banner carrier on the same daily rate of pay as an archer'.

THE JOLLY ROGER WAS A PIRATE FLAG

The pirates of old who infested the high seas were not the jolly, bluff characters projected by the adventure stories. Nor were they so honourable as to fly a flag publicising their trade to one and all, thus giving warning to any potential victim who might get in a couple of well-placed shots first.

In earlier days most nations issued what they called Letters of Marque to any privateer who wanted one, such documents permitting the holder to fly the flag of the issuing nation and plunder her enemies' ships for a split of the proceeds. In practice most privateers would have a go at any ship that crossed their path and, clad in the thin veneer of their Letter of Marque, behaved little better than the worst of the pirates. Austria, having no navy to speak of, issued these documents like confetti and so a very high proportion of such scum flew the Imperial black spread eagle with two heads against a yellow background and, from a distance, this would sufficiently resemble a skull and cross-bones to get tales of such a flag started. The first hysterical ravings of pirates flying such a gruesome calling-card certainly told of such a colour scheme instead of the now traditional black and white.

As for the name 'Jolly Roger', that at least has some foundation in fact, but subsequently became ensnared in the realm of myth. Known not only to privateers but to regular ships of most navies was a plain red duster which, if hoisted prior to battle, was intended as and understood to mean that no quarter would be expected or accepted; a fight to the death, in other words. The French name for that flag was the Jolie Rouge.

JOSEPH HAD A COAT OF MANY COLOURS

Unfortunately for the popular musical, Joseph never had any such garment, not according to the original scriptures. The original Hebrew states the garment to be 'a long garment with sleeves', but makes no mention of colour at all.

K

KAMIKAZE ATTACKS AND THEIR EFFECTIVENESS

Albeit highly apposite to the Westerner's idea of the mentality of the Japanese, who did seem to spend most of the Second World War wandering around in search of an honourable end, there never was the mass volunteering for this particular brand of lunacy that popular belief maintains. After Vice-Admiral Ohnishi had come up with the bright idea, he was fortunate enough to find a few pilots stupid enough to volunteer to go and try the plan out and assess its practicalities. Quite how they reported back is unclear, but their mission was considered to have been sufficiently successful to justify the implementation of the concept on a large scale. The only problem was that further volunteers, like the pioneers of the idea, were extremely thin on the ground.

To a man, the pilots of the 2,314 Kamikaze squads that flew were all pressed into the job.

The effectiveness of the Kamikaze squads is highly debatable. The colossal psychological impact upon the objectives cannot be denied. In a wartime situation, Westerners basically fought to stay alive and, not unnaturally, found themselves more than a little bemused by the reverse. Still, most of the pilots were, by virtue of their selection, expendable to say the least. They were, for the most part, young and almost totally untrained, and the planes that they flew were typically outdated and fit for the scrap heap. It soon became standard practice for one experienced pilot to lead his flock to the target zone and leave them to it. En route, the group would have to stay at the speed of the slowest, thus leaving themselves vulnerable to fighter attack and, once at the target zone, they were shot down fairly easily being unskilled in evasive tactics. As already said, the Japanese launched 2,314 missions, some comprising over 300 planes, but although they damaged quite a few ships, they only managed to sink thirty-four – a direct hit from a kamikaze was by no means a ticket to Davy Jones's locker. In other words, considering the number of planes involved, the success rate is hardly impressive.

The term 'kamikaze' was taken from a famous incident in Japanese history when a typhoon destroyed a massive fleet sent against them by the Mongol Empire. Considering this to be the result of divine intervention, the Japanese named the wind 'Kami Kaze' – meaning divine wind. History does not record what the Mongols called it!

'KISS ME HARDY'

Despite the notion that long periods at sea are apt to warp a chap, these were not the last words of Nelson as he lay dying. What he most likely said was, 'Kismet,

Hardy', and this was either misheard due to the noise of battle, or misunderstood by some nearby. Kismet is not just fate, but the fulfilment of destiny or the culmination of one's preordained journey through life.

KRAKATOA LIES EAST OF JAVA AND IS THE SITE OF THE WORLD'S LARGEST VOLCANIC ERUPTION

It may have been the loudest explosion ever heard, but far larger than the eruption of Krakatoa in 1883 was that of Tambora on Sumbawa Island in 1815. In that year alone, an estimated minimum of 150 million tons of ash were discharged into the atmosphere out of a total discharge of 220 million tons between 1811 and 1818. Krakatoa only managed some 50 million tons.

Actually, Krakatoa lies due west of Java in the Sundra Strait, not east as is commonly believed; a misconception so deeply rooted that it is enshrined in the title of the feature film, 'Krakatoa, East of Java'. Tambora lies east of Java, so perhaps this gave rise to the confusion.

THE KREMLIN

The media are almost wholly responsible for promoting the idea that there is only one Kremlin in Russia and that it is the name of a specific building in Moscow. 'Kremlin' is an ordinary noun, not a proper one, and describes a walled complex, not an individual building. Many Russian cities have a kremlin.

L

LANCELOT AND HIS INVOLVEMENT WITH THE ROUND TABLE

It is at best a matter of conjecture whether there was even a King Arthur of the Britons, but one thing is certain — in the original Arthurian legends there was no mention whatsoever of a knight named Lancelot.

Many sources maintain that his origin lies in the twelfth-century work of the French writer Chrétien de Troyes but, although Lancelot undoubtedly entered English literature this way, his ultimate origin lies in the ancient European god known to the Romans as Lugus. With various name changes, he emerged in several cultures as the ultimate macho hero of saga and legend, a sort of medieval medallion-man.

For his work on the life and times of King Arthur, Sir Thomas Mallory drew on several sources and lifted Lancelot wholesale from French literature and 'slotted' him in to beef up the tales with daring deeds and romance. That Mallory chose to write in such a character is hardly surprising for he was far from the genteel old scholar that many imagine him to have been. He first came to prominance in 1450 due to his involvement in an unsuccessful attempt to assassinate the Duke of Buckingham. His colourful career included robbery, extortion, cattle rustling, rape and plundering monasteries. From time to time, England felt the need of a rest from Sir Thomas and his little peccadillos, so he was locked up in some castle or other for a spell. It was during these enforced rests from his taxing hobbies that he wrote his books.

LEAD IS THE HEAVIEST METAL
Lead is a long way short of fitting this description. Gold, mercury and tungsten are just three of the many that have a much greater density.

LEAP YEARS OCCUR EVERY FOUR YEARS
This is by no means the determining rule. Leap years occur only if the year in question is divisible by four, or by 400 if it is a centenary. 1900, for example, was divisible by four but did not qualify as a leap year since it did not divide equally by 400. The year 2000 will qualify being divisible by both.

LEMMINGS AND THEIR SO-CALLED MASS SUICIDE
The popular superstition regarding these Arctic rodents is that, every now and again, they embark upon a mass suicide drive into the sea which heralds an impending catastrophe of international implication. The reality is somewhat less mystical, for the only thing that drives the lemming is hunger.

Lemmings do swarm periodically but do so in search of food; there is no great carpet of lemmings scurrying inexorably to the cliffs where they hurl themselves into the sea and drown. There wouldn't be so many little lemmings if they did! When they move out of their established feeding grounds, depleted by overpopulation, they do so in a radial pattern and like to follow established paths, be they made by man or animal. They do seem to have a natural dislike of water and will undertake any diversion to avoid crossing it; something that they will only do when it is absolutely necessary. Few of the marches ever lead as far as the sea, but when they do, some of the lemmings fail to recognise the sea as such and, thinking it to be only an expanse of water that cannot be detoured, swim so far out that they become exhausted and drown. The majority simply about turn or hang around the beach area pondering their next move.

LEPROSY IS A HIGHLY CONTAGIOUS DISEASE

Not only is this untrue, but a high number of people have a natural immunity to the condition. Those who are not possessed of this natural protection require a great deal more than superficial contact with a leper to become infected. A sustained and intimate contact and association should do the trick, but even that cannot be guaranteed to produce a positive result. If all the misconceptions about leprosy were true, there would not be a single doctor or nurse left working in the field uncontaminated.

The hideous deformities that are the favourites of the make-up departments of film companies making biblical epics, are essentially a thing of the past and only now arise if an infected person ignores the initial symptoms and does not seek medical aid for years afterwards. Nowadays, patients undergoing treatment largely live at home and carry on with their normal working lives.

On the subject of leprosy and the Bible, it is more than doubtful that the disease mentioned therein is anything like the one bearing the name today, since the term used to be bandied around to cover a multitude of sins including, in all probability, syphilis. It is true that the term 'leprosy' does appear in the Authorised Version of the Bible, but scholars consider this to be a poor translation of the Hebrew *tsaraath* – a general term for skin disorders.

'LET THEM EAT CAKE'

This, the best known 'quotation' from French history, is invariably and erroneously attributed to Marie Antoinette; the Revolutionaries maintaining that she said it during the Paris Bread Riots of 5 and 6 October 1789. What is fairly certain is that the Duchesse de Polignac, a close friend of the Queen, said to her, 'How is it that these silly people are so clamorous for bread when they can buy such nice brioches for a few sous?' – brioche being a kind of sponge cake. As for the curt 'Let them eat cake' – it had already been said in 1739, which was sixteen years before Marie Antoinette was even born. In Jean Jacques Rousseau's *Confessions*, published in 1766, he makes reference to the Grenoble Bread Riots of 1739, and says that: 'A great princess callously remarked, "Let them eat cake." ' The truth of the matter is that the Revolutionaries circulated the rumour that Marie Antoinette had said such a thing to discredit her further with the people – not a difficult task.

LIE DETECTORS AND TRUTH DRUGS

Neither of these interrogation aids is anything like as effective or efficient as the image of them projected by the film business, where they nearly always work. Lie detectors monitor factors such as blood pressure, respiration rate, skin conductivity and pulse rate in an attempt to establish stress patterns that might indicate that the subject is lying. Anyone with a considerable amount of self-control can easily fool such a machine, and a pathological liar who believes his own stories certainly could.

To a certain extent, the so-called truth drugs are only as good as the interrogator. It is extremely easy to lead the subject inadvertently off on a tangent – even to false confession due to a deep-rooted guilt complex. Many people have been found to be highly suggestible in the twilight sleep induced by such drugs as scopolamine, and evidence based on information so extracted is inadmissible in court.

LIGHTNING NEVER STRIKES IN THE SAME PLACE TWICE

Since lightning takes the most straightforward and convenient route to earth, i.e. the nearest, tallest and conductive structure, this assertion is patently untrue. Providing that the structure in question is not reduced in height by a previous strike and is no longer the highest in the locality, it will be the most likely target in the next storm as well. There are numerous towers and high buildings that sustain repeated lightning strikes – the C.N. Tower in Toronto averages over 200 hits per year.

The general concepts of the very nature of lightning and its method and patterns of movement are pretty wide of the truth. For a start, it does not zigzag down to earth – nature chooses far more direct paths for it to follow. Nor are the brilliant flashes seen actually racing down from the clouds to the surface of the earth. What you in fact see is lightning discharging itself from the ground back to the sky. The leader stroke that jumps from the cloud down to the earth is of a very low luminosity and rarely exceeds 1,000 miles per second. The 'positive giant' return stroke occurs almost simultaneously, and it is this that people see as it sears its way up to the sky at speeds approaching 90,000 miles per second, causing compression waves that are heard as thunder. Despite its presenting an aurora measurable in feet, the core of a lightning strike is no more than half an inch in diameter, yet holds temperatures of up to 54,000° F.

In real terms, there is no such thing as sheet lightning. It is ordinary lightning seen at a great distance or discharging itself inside a cloud thus diffusing a blanket of light.

As a side-note, it was lightning that started the old belief in thunderbolts. Given its colossal temperature, lightning striking, shall we say, a water saturated tree or rock, will boil that water instantaneously, causing violent and rapid expansion resulting in a shattering effect. The overall impression is that of the target having been struck by a powerful physical force.

LINDBERG WAS THE FIRST MAN TO FLY THE ATLANTIC

Perhaps it was the remorseless American publicity machine that ensured that any time anyone thinks of the early transatlantic flights, the name of Charles Lindberg leaps to mind. Far from being the first, Lindberg was the seventy-ninth. It was in May of 1919 that Lt Commander Read became the first man to fly the Atlantic. Piloting a United States Navy flying boat, he broke his journey at the Azores before continuing to land at Plymouth. The first non-stop flight came in June of the same year when Alcock and Brown made their trip. All this happened eight years before Lindberg made his solo flight.

THE LONGBOW AS AN ENGLISH INVENTION

As famous as our archers made this formidable weapon, it is of Welsh design and invention, not English. Nor was it the advent of gunpowder and muskets that heralded the end of the days of the supremacy of the knights – it was the advent of the longbow. Massed arrow fire could devastate armoured cavalry every time, as we proved to the French to the point of insult.

Nor did the coming of the early muskets sound the death knell for the bow, which remained a superior weapon for many a year. It had a much higher rate of fire, accuracy and reliability.

LUCIFER AS A NAME FOR THE DEVIL

The Bible makes no such association! The name appears only once in the whole book, and then only as an epithet for Nebuchadrezzar (note the spelling, it is '-rezzar' and not '-nezzar'), the fallen king of Babylon. The relevant passages occur in Isaiah 14: 12–15: 'How art thou fallen from heaven, O Lucifer, son of the morning. . . For thou hast said in thine heart, I will ascend into heaven, I will exalt my throne above the stars of God. . . Yet thou shalt be brought down to hell.'

A quick trip to the Bible will reveal that Isaiah is crowing over the fall of the pagan king, and the employment of the name Lucifer is, in all probability, a piece of sarcasm. Be that as it may, it is nevertheless a logical choice to use in conjunction with 'Son of the morning', since the name means 'lightbringing'. The overall description of the collapse of Nebuchadrezzar does sound very much like the popular, yet erroneous idea about the fall of Satan, who was not kicked out of heaven and cast down to Hell for the sin of false pride; he lost a power struggle with Michael, which is hardly the same thing. It would appear that this confusion was enough to bring the name into disrepute. This confusion must be of relatively recent development since there was a famous Bishop Lucifer in the fourth century who is still regarded as a saint in Sardinia.

So strong is this erroneous association, that it is extremely unlikely that any Church would permit the christening of a boy child with the name. Strangely enough, there are no such prejudices attached to all the female equivalents like Lucy, Lucinda or Lucille, all of which, like Lucifer, derive from *lux*, the Latin for light.

LUSITANIA – MYTHS REGARDING HER SINKING

Many assume the ship to have been American, since the most oft heard myth regarding her sinking is that the incident brought America into the First World War. America made a lot of noise; Theodore Roosevelt made all the right sort of outraged condemnations of Germany – 'piracy' and all that, and then let the matter slide. The *Lusitania* was torpedoed on 7 May 1915, which was two years before America joined in the war. She was a British liner and out of the death toll of 1,198 only some 120 odd were Americans.

As to the ship having been an innocent passenger liner torpedoed without warning, this is a long way from the truth. The Germans had issued numerous warnings, both verbal and written. On the very day the *Lusitania* sailed from New York, the German government took space on the front page of the *New York World* to reiterate their warning that they had mounted a blockade of the British Isles. In that notice, which they had placed pointedly right next to Cunard's announcement of the imminent departure of the *Lusitania*, they gave warning that any vessel attempting to run that blockade would find itself the target of submarine attack. The message could hardly have been clearer.

The Cunard executives took the warnings seriously enough; they ordered the *Lusitania*'s captain to assume a zigzag sailing pattern on the homeward journey, and to avoid all landfalls. For reasons best known to the captain himself, he chose to ignore both these instructions and was holding a steady course at the reduced speed of twenty-one knots as he, again contrary to instructions, passed near the Old Head of Kinsale in southern Ireland. In this manner, he presented a sitting target to the captain of the U-20 who took full advantage of the situation. U-20 scored two direct hits and, after her boilers blew, the *Lusitania* went rapidly to the bottom.

As for her not being a legitimate military target, this is at best a matter of interpretation. She was carrying a goodly number of Canadian volunteeers, 5,000 cases of munitions and a consignment of fulminate of mercury fuses. All said and done, we had been at war with Germany for over ten months at the time so, without any disrespect to the near 1,200 who went down with her, it is rather difficult to see what the righteous indignation was all about.

At the end of the day it comes down to who wins the war and writes the history books. I mean, everyone has heard about the sinking of the *Lusitania*, but how many know about the sinking of the unarmed German liner *Wilhelm Gustloff* in 1945 which killed nearly 8,000 women and children.

M

MACADAM ROADS
'Macadam' is not synonymous with 'asphalt'; the term designates a road construction method, not a surfacing material.

John Macadam (1756–1836) developed a method of road building that relied on a firm subsoil packed with large pieces of rock, which was subsequently covered with a layer of small pieces of broken stone. To finish the whole thing off, a layer of fine gravel and crushed slag was used to fill in all the gaps. It was not until 1854 that a Nottingham-based surveyor named Hooley initiated the use of tar as a road-surfacing material, he calling it 'tarmacadam' in Macadam's honour. Later trade names like 'Tarmac' helped to cement the notion that macadam and tarmacadam were one and the same thing.

MACBETH MURDERED DUNCAN FOR THE THRONE OF SCOTLAND

Only in Shakespeare's play, and Shakespeare was never one to let historical fact or basic credibility stand in the way of a good yarn. In real life, Duncan died in open combat on the battlefield in the year 1040. Neither was Macbeth the conniving usurper of Shakespeare's imagination. He had a perfectly good claim to the throne – at least as good as Duncan's, if not better according to some authorities.

MAD AS A HATTER

The usual theory attached to the origin of this expression maintains that prolonged contact with the mercurous nitrates used in the hatting trade gave rise to a condition not unlike St Vitus's dance. However, the expression was in use in a slightly altered form long before hat-making was an organised trade and, indeed, before the chemical was used. Lewis Carroll popularised the phrase in *Alice in Wonderland*, the context in which he used it giving false backing to the false derivation.

The saying was originally 'mad as an atter' – *atter* being Anglo-Saxon for an adder. 'Mad' is being used here to mean injurious or poisonous, so the true meaning of the expression is 'as dangerous as an adder'. Although we no longer use the word 'mad' in any other context than that of insanity, this does not hold true in America. Isolated from the seat of English, 'mad' remains in current American usage where it means really angry and potentially dangerous. 'Fall' (q.v.) is another example of long-lost English surviving in America.

MAD AS A MARCH HARE

As with the previous entry, this is a hand-me-down bastardisation of the original. The proper form is 'mad as a marsh hare' and there are many examples of the same in early literature. The Dutch scholar Desiderius Erasmus (1466–1536) used the saying in his publication entitled *Aphorisms*, explaining that: 'Hares are wilder in the marshes from the absence of hedges and cover.' In other words, when hares moved across the open reaches of marshlands, they felt exposed and vulnerable and therefore tended to spring in wild and erratic patterns.

MAGELLAN, DRAKE, AND THE FIRST CIRCUMNAVIGATION

Magellan was killed in the Philippines in 1521 before he could complete the second leg of his attempted circumnavigation. The relatively unknown Juan Sebastian del Cano, a member of Magellan's expedition, completed the return to Seville, thereby qualifying as the first man to achieve this feat. Drake did not begin his voyage until 1577, thus becoming the first Englishman to undertake it. Unlike the Magellan expedition, which sailed halfway round the world in one direction and then the other, Drake travelled in one direction only.

MAGI MYTHS

The fact that only the gospel attributed to Matthew bothers to mention the Star of Bethlehem, and the men that are supposed to have followed it, must cast a long shadow of doubt across the authenticity of the events themselves for, not only is Matthew's word unreliable (see also JESUS THE CHRIST WAS BORN IN A STABLE IN BETHLEHEM ON 25 DECEMBER 1 BC) but, if such did occur, surely it would have been of sufficient importance to merit a mention in at least one of the other gospels. Anyway, even leaving all that to one side, there are more than one or two misconceptions attached to the tradition itself.

To begin with, the men making up the delegation

weren't kings and, secondly, nobody knows how many they were because Matthew neglects to say. In the second century AD, the theologian Origen pronounced, off his own bat, that the number of dignitaries had been three. He was, presumably, working on the basis that there had only been three different types of gift, but there's nothing to say that any number of men within the delegation didn't turn up bearing, for example, gold. By the sixth century AD, a great deal more importance had been placed on the visit of the Magi – that being the title of an ancient priestly caste of Persia. Bede decided that they really ought to be more elevated, so he not only promoted them to kingship, but he also bestowed the now traditional fancy names of Melchior, Gaspar and Balthazar.

Next we have the romantic image of the three kindly old monarchs following a guiding star across the desert to the stable in Bethlehem. Not according to the Bible we haven't! Matthew tells us that the Magi saw a heavenly body rise in the east, which prompted them to travel west to Jerusalem – hardly following at all. Upon their arrival in that city, they went straight to the court of Herod to inquire where the Christ was supposed to be born. After consulting his prophets, the King told them to go to Bethlehem, and it was on this last leg of the journey that they supposedly held the star in sight, but, since they were already well aware of their destination, it is quite fair to say that they did not actually follow the star at any point on their journey.

Innumerable religious paintings and countless Nativity plays have compounded into longevity the error that the Magi visited the 'stable' immediately after the birth. Only the shepherds turned up at the birth scene; the Magi visited the 'young child' Jesus in 'the house' and, if anything in the Bible can be regarded as historically or chronologically accurate, there must have been a gap of at least two years between the two events because of

Herod supposedly ordering the death of all children up to the age of two after the Magi had passed through his court. Again, it is only Matthew who mentions this extraordinary event, there being no other mention of such in any contemporary writings, which is strange to say the least. Either way, the Church recognises the events as being separate and divided by a considerable time-span, which is why they celebrate the visitation by the Magi with Epiphany on 6 January.

MAN HAS THE LARGEST BRAIN OF ALL THE PRIMATES IN PROPORTION TO BODY SIZE

Man must have come a long way since his primitive breast-beating days for he likes to take false pride in the above myth, whilst at the same time coyly, yet mistakenly, attributing the greatest proportional penis size of all primates to the mighty gorilla. Unfortunately for man, who now seeks intellectual superiority, he is condemned to carry the biggest penis but not the biggest brain; that distinction goes to the common marmoset of east Brazil. In fact, with the blue whale's brain constituting a paltry 0.007 per cent of the animal's body weight, the elephant 0.125 per cent, and man a pitiful 1.93 per cent, the marmoset, with a brain accounting for 5.55 of its body weight, can claim the highest body/brain ratio of any mammal.

Within humans the brain size does vary with age, sex and race. Dare it be said in these days of female militancy, but women's brains are quite significantly smaller than those found in men. It is also true that Negro brains are on average some 40 cc smaller than Whites' but, before any racists or MCPs take false comfort in this, it must be stated that not only does brain size have little to do with brain power (Neanderthal man's brain was about 100 cc larger than ours), but the brains of the American Indian, the

Eskimo, the Kaffirs and the Japanese are generally larger than those found in Whites. It is also worth stating to be a fiction the notion that Negro skulls are significantly thicker than Europeans' in order to afford the owners additional protection to the brain from the sun.

MANNA FROM HEAVEN

According to the book of Numbers 2: 4–6, the 'children of Israel' were not at all impressed with God's supposed gift of manna; it appears to have been far from the joyous salvation that the general impression of the event suggests. The recipients spent all their time moaning about the fish and fruit that they used to get so freely in Egypt, and complaining about how vile the manna tasted – which, to be fair, it does! All said and done, the Israelites did not regard the 'manna from heaven' in any way similar to the meaning of the expression today.

Not unnaturally, God was a trifle put out at their ingratitude and told them so in no uncertain terms. He also told them that, just to teach them a lesson, they would have to go on eating the filthy stuff until 'it comes out of your nostrils.' So, it was a punishment in the end, not a blessing.

Actually, it is quite unfair to blame or praise divine intervention for the appearance of the manna since it has, throughout the Middle East and Asia from the beginning of time, turned up every year. A plant called *Tamarix Gallica* exudes a highly nutritious secretion via perforations made in it by certain insects around June and July. The 'manna' is collected as it solidifies in the cool morning air, and is gathered up as easily today as it would have been in biblical times.

MARRIAGE AT SEA BY THE SHIP'S CAPTAIN IS LEGAL

So firmly entrenched in the popular imagination is the romantic notion of a shipboard love affair culminating in a marriage performed by the ship's captain on a moonlit deck, that it is going to take more than this book to unseat it. Nevertheless, no ships' captains, of this or any other nation, have the power to perform a wedding ceremony. Furthermore, they are strongly advised not to allow such a ceremony to take place aboard their vessels, even if presided over by a fully ordained minister of the church. Imagine if you can, the legal complications if, for example, a Frenchman and a Spanish woman were married by an Italian priest whilst aboard a British vessel that happened to be in Greek waters at the time. Where, if anywhere, would the marriage have legal status?

MATA HARI WAS A BEAUTIFUL, YOUNG ORIENTAL SPY

She wasn't young; she wasn't oriental; Mata Hari was not her real name; that she was a 'spy' in the proper sense of the word is wholly untenable, and there is significant doubt as to whether or not she ever trafficked in intelligence at all, and, with all due respect to the famous lady herself, she wasn't even beautiful.

Born Margaretha Gertrude Zelle, she was of Dutch parentage and subsequently married a Dutch army officer of Scottish extraction who just happened to be serving in the Dutch East Indies. There is some confusion as to whether she and her husband separated in Java or shortly after their joint return to Europe, but, whichever it was, she re-emerged and found employment as an 'exotic danseuse'. She also seems to have exhausted more French officers than did the entire war effort, but neither of these two things makes her the young, sylph-like vamp of popular imagination; there is a world of difference between being attractive to men and simply being available, and the clubs where she plied her 'art' were not exactly top-line. Then as now, there were still plenty of places willing to stage living proof of the old adage that some women over 40 (she was a plump, middle-aged divorcee nudging 42 when shot) are like salads in that both are better dressed.

Now working under the stage-name of Mata Hari, that being a poetic Malay phrase to describe the sun which roughly translates as 'eye of the day', she came to this country in the November of 1916, and was arrested by British Intelligence officers aboard the SS *Hollandia* as it lay in Falmouth harbour bound for Holland. The arresting agents had got her completely mixed up with a known German agent named Carla Benedix and, after the mix-up was realised, they let her go but notified the French anyway. When she finally got back to France in February 1917, she was arrested.

Zelle herself claims it was the French Secret Service that had approached her with the request that she gather intelligence for them when she made a trip to German-occupied Belgium, but the British *allegedly* informed the French that she had been recruited by the Germans when in The Hague in the spring of 1916. All in all it would appear that the trial was a mere formality in a political face-saving operation in which Zelle was the patient who unfortunately did not survive. She was shot in July 1917 and went to the land of myth.

MEDIEVAL PEOPLE WERE MIDGETS

Suits of armour on display in museums and castles are mainly responsible for this myth. When so viewed, a suit of armour is, for want of a better word, collapsed, in that the flexible leather junctions and gussets between the metal plates are relaxed. When actually worn, the suit would accommodate a man at least six or seven inches taller than the 'collapsed' height.

METAPHYSICS

Words and phrases like 'metaphysical', 'transcendental meditation', and 'self-realisation' walked hand in hand through the superficial sixties and seventies. They were constantly being trotted out by pop groups and folk singers who thought that everything in life should be free – except their records and the seats at their concerts. Metaphysics, to anyone who has ever taken the trouble to look in the dictionary, does not have any association at all with things spiritual, mystical or pseudo-religious. The OED states that the term 'came to be misinterpreted as meaning the science of things transcending what is physical or natural'.

The word first appeared as a posthumously bestowed title for a work of Aristotle's which chronologically followed his publication entitled *Physics*. 'Metaphysics' simply means after, or following, 'Physics'. The work dealt with the basic principles of existence, e.g. substance, reality and essence, which is about as far from its current application as it is possible to get.

MICE LOVE CHEESE

Everyone knows that this is true so perhaps someone ought to tell the mice as well. In all experiments they have persistently failed to demonstrate any preference for cheese at all. Sweets are, it would seem, their favourite food.

MOHICANS AND PUNK HAIR STYLES

Chingachook must be turning in his grave at his once proud people's name being fallaciously associated with the far from attractive craze of punks. A Mohican looked like the standard issue 'Cowboy and Indian' Indian; his hair style resembled that of the hippies of the sixties rather than anything else. The only possible explanation for the mistake is the wealth of films made about 'Hawkeye' and the 'Last of the Mohicans'. All these films feature a large number of Huron Indians who fought the French and did sport the 'Trojan plume' hairdo so favoured by the deranged devotees of punk. 'Huron' is the French for 'bristle-head'. Since there was such a large number of Hurons and only two Mohican Indians, people seem to have got confused with their Indians.

MONEY IS THE ROOT OF ALL EVIL
Another of the great all-time misquotes, which was presumably corrupted by the poor to counteract their envy of the rich. The First Epistle of Timothy 6: 10, actually states: 'For the love of money is the root of all evil.'

'MONGOOSE' AND ITS PLURAL
The accepted plural of this creature's name is 'mongooses', not 'mongeese' or even the more exotic 'mongi', which is occasionally put forward. Nor is the mongoose immune to the venom of the snakes that it kills, as the less fleet of foot of the species have found out.

MONKEYS GROOM EACH OTHER FOR FLEAS
When visitors to the zoo see monkeys picking through each other's fur and eating what they find, they usually assume the above to be true. But monkeys do not host fleas in their natural habitat nor do they in zoos, for they are far too clean and active to attract them in the first

place. When they scour each other's coats, they are looking for small particles of dried skin and deposits of a salty secretion that sometimes exudes from their skin. If anything, monkeys are far more likely to catch parasites from the visitors than the other way round.

MOTHER SHIPTON, NOSTRADAMUS, AND THEIR SO CALLED PROPHECIES

It is a matter of individual choice whether or not to believe that there are those amongst us who can gaze out across the centuries and foretell with terrifying accuracy the things that are yet to come. Be that as it may, there never was any Mother Shipton and most of her better-known prophecies were made up by others centuries after her 'death'.

Supposedly born in a cave in Knaresborough, York-shire, in 1488, she was baptised Ursula Southiel but later married one Tobias Shipton. The myth of Mother Shipton first reared its head in 1641 in a tract that declared she had foretold many things, including the lives and deaths of, amongst others, Thomas Cromwell and Cardinal Wolsey. Whoever it was that concocted this tract was not overly adventurous since he only accredited her with foretelling events between her supposed death and 1641; in other words, the forger stuck to things that had already happened so that he could be sure of his historical facts. So, whoever he was, he did not attempt any vicarious crystal gazing; but others did.

All the nonsense about her having foretold the telegraph, steam engines, submarines and metal ships derives from 'prophecies' written for her by a London-based publisher and bookdealer named Charles Hindley. He issued his forgery in 1862 only to admit all in 1873. One of Hindley's forgeries said that the world was going to come to an end in 1881 and, despite his fairly well-publicised confession eight years before, that year saw the gullible and the superstitious quitting their homes in droves to spend their last days in prayer in the fields, only to feel cheated by the continuance of their lives. Perhaps they were not that stupid, for there are those today who prefer to believe that a fifteenth-century prophet/peasant had foreseen all.

Much the same sort of thing happened to the writings of Nostradamus. Through the centuries, his collection of forecasts, itself entitled *Centuries*, has been bent, twisted and 'interpreted' by numerous people. As recently as 1940, Hitler was showering Europe with 'Nostradamus' leaflets stating that the prophet had foretold the Third Reich and that Germany was on a preordained mission to save the world from itself. Not to be outdone, the Allies immediately set about inventing Nostradamus prophecies forecasting supreme and glorious victory.

People are forever stating that Nostradamus foretold this, that or the other, but if you go back to the original text nothing of the sort is to be found. He was extremely careful to be as obscure as possible so that he could mean all things to all men. He wrote in a bizarre mixture of various languages that included Old French and Latin; he also resorted to symbols and anagrams. In short, you could make the long-dead prophet say anything that you wanted him to. It is very difficult to be accused of being hopelessly wrong if no one is sure as to what you said in the first place.

MUTINY ON THE BOUNTY

No matter how laudable Charles Laughton's performance was of a draconian ship's master who drove his poor downtrodden crew reluctantly to mutiny, the facts of the voyage are somewhat different.

Bligh was not a demented disciplinarian and Christian was not a philanthropic young man concerned with the lot of his social inferiors. The two men were close friends, not enemies, in fact, Christian was Bligh's protégé, encouraged and aided by his friend at every step of his career. The last help up the ladder had occurred on the outward bound leg of the *Bounty*'s fateful voyage, when Bligh promoted Christian from master's mate to acting Lieutenant. This would indicate that all was well between the two men who had sailed together twice before.

For some reason, relationships deteriorated rapidly after their arrival at Tahiti. Some of the more lurid speculation about the cause of this concerns the disruption of their supposed homosexual affair after Christian fell for the charms of the less-than-shy island girls. Whatever the cause, it would seem that the subsequent mutiny was simply the culmination of a fierce personality clash between the two men. With what Tahiti had to offer sailors, it can't have been hard for Christian to incite the bulk of the crew to rebel. Taking Bligh's ship away from him would have been the ultimate insult, and there is much evidence that Christian was behaving in a sufficiently unbalanced manner to go that far just to get one over on his old friend.

The rest is history, but there is one last misconception attached to the events – the mutiny did not bring a halt to Bligh's career. He led quite a distinguished life, at one time serving as Governor of New South Wales where, unfortunately, he wound up in the middle of another mutiny in 1808. He retired in 1814 with the rank of Vice-Admiral.

'MY CUP RUNNETH OVER'

Perhaps it was the translators' enthusiasm for the sentiment that caused this exaggerated corruption of the original Hebrew which simply said, 'My cup is full.'

N

NELSON DISOBEYED ORDERS AT THE BATTLE OF COPENHAGEN

Nelson may have been many things but a cavalier rebel against command he most certainly was not. Some time before Admiral Sir Hyde Parker, who was in command of the British fleet at the battle, raised the signal telling those ships engaged with the enemy to discontinue action, he had sent his Flag Captain, named Otway, to Nelson with the verbal message that, should such a signal be raised, then he, Nelson, could read it as permissive. In other words, it was an 'out' for Nelson if he wanted it. Being the man on the spot and therefore best suited to judge, Nelson was free to continue the engagement or retreat, and Parker would assume responsibility either way.

The fiasco with the telescope to the blind eye was merely a joke at the expense of the nearby Colonel Stewart, who was totally unaware of the verbal overrider to the orders brought by Otway. The navy never could resist a dig at the army!

O

'O ROMEO, ROMEO, WHEREFORE ART THOU ROMEO?'

Many have been the comedy sketches in which Juliet utters these immortal words from a balcony whilst shading her eyes and scouring the landscape for her Romeo who is threshing about in the shrubbery beneath. Apart from being overplayed, this sort of buffoonery only serves to fuel the misunderstanding of the line by the general public. 'Wherefore' in this context does not mean 'where'; in the days when the play was written it meant 'why'. Since the lovers' families were at loggerheads and thwarting the desired union, Juliet is in fact asking Romeo why he has to be Romeo; why couldn't he be someone else to whom her family would not object.

OCTANES AND PERFORMANCE

The best known and most widely used octane, or anti-knock, is the now infamous tetraethyl lead. Its function is to prevent premature combustion of the fuel by small, local areas of high pressure inside the cylinder, before the piston has reached a point just after 'top dead centre' – the correct position for it to receive the impact of the power stroke. Detonation of the fuel before TDC causes various parts of the engine to fight against each other, and this generates a metallic knocking sound.

Anti-knock is the additive's only function; the phrase 'high octane' has no connotations of performance, purity or strength. Four star petrol is not somehow better than two star – for a lot of engines it would be worse. Each model of engine has a specific octane requirement which, when satisfied, enables that motor to function at peak efficiency. Buying additional and unnecessary octanes will not make your car go any faster; just your money.

OCTOPUS AND SQUID EJECT INK TO HIDE BEHIND

Not only is the amount discharged too small to conceal the animal concerned, but the cloud is not designed to disperse – just the opposite. Both creatures produce individual patterns each consistent with their own body shapes. The ink is released in such a way as to produce a 'doppelganger' to confuse an aggressor who, hopefully, attacks the ghost while the real animal makes its getaway. The ink also has the effect of deadening the olfactory senses of the attacker, which adds to the confusion.

OCTOPUSES CRUSH THINGS WITH THEIR TENTACLES

The animal is equipped with suction pads on its tentacles, and it is with these that it grips its prey while it bites it with its parrot-like beak. Only in cartoons and submarine fantasies do its tentacles behave like aquatic anacondas.

'OLYMPIAD' DENOTES AN OLYMPIC MEETING

With all the cheating, drug abuse, political infighting and the ever-present threat of terrorist activity, which at Munich became a sick reality, it is rather daft to refer to these meetings as games; but that's another matter. When President Reagan opened the 1984 Hollywood-style fiasco, he declared the 'twenty-third Olympiad open', which would be a little difficult since 'olympiad' refers to the span of four years between each meeting.

THE OLYMPIC FLAME IS A TRADITION WITH ITS ROOTS IN ANTIQUITY

Although the notion of an undying flame is one of great antiquity – it most likely survived as a hangover from the days when man had not yet learned the techniques of making fire and had to keep alive that which was given to him by natural phenomena – the Olympic torch has no such age. It must be the only thing for which the present civilisation has to thank A. Hitler Esq, for it was he, and he alone, who came up with the idea for the

1936 Berlin games. An impressive relay of international runners was organised to carry the flame all the way from Athens to Berlin. Who knows, perhaps the Olympic flame may yet burn for a thousand years.

'ON THE WHOLE, I'D RATHER BE IN PHILADELPHIA'

Although himself a native of this much maligned city, W.C. Fields never missed a chance to have a crack at the place, but it is untrue that the above is inscribed on his gravestone which simply reads – 'W.C. FIELDS 1880–1946'.

'ONE SMALL STEP FOR MAN'

Unfortunately for posterity, Commander Neil Armstrong of the Apollo 11 moonshot fluffed his lines on that historic moment which, given the strain that he was no doubt under, is altogether understandable. What he should have said was: 'That is one small step for *a* man, one giant leap for mankind.' All very moving stuff, to be sure. Without the preposition 'a', 'man' on its own means 'mankind', so, when Armstrong actually said, 'That's one small step for man, one giant leap for mankind', his utterance was at best contradictory and at worst totally nonsensical.

'ONE TOUCH OF NATURE MAKES THE WHOLE WORLD KIN'

Far from meaning that all humanity is united under the hand of Mother Nature, this line from 'Troilus and Cressida' which is invariably taken out of context, is actually an observation on the shallowness of human nature. In Act 3, Scene 3, Ulysses says, 'One touch of nature makes the whole world kin,/That all with one consent praise new-born gawds.' 'Gawds' meant insignificant trifles of no real merit, and what the whole speech boils down to is that if there is one universal fault with people, it is that they, like magpies, are invariably attracted to that which glistens, not that which is real gold.

ONLY BLACKS WERE ENSLAVED IN AMERICA

It was the Spanish who started the trade of black slaves to the New World, not the British settlers. This did not stop many an Englishman making a fortune out of the disgusting business, but the facts of the matter are that the first boatload of misery arrived in 1516, which was 120 years before the *Mayflower* landed.

Before going outside the country for slaves, the Spanish tried using the American Indian, but he proved to be mentally unsuited; in fact, he would rather sit down and be starved or beaten to death before he would submit to the indignities of manual labour and servitude which, as far as he was concerned, were strictly for women and animals. And he was a warrior!

Nor were all the Blacks in America at that time slaves. Many were freemen operating in private business, often as slave traders. All successful black families had house slaves, but legislation was passed in 1670 to prohibit Blacks owning white slaves because this was considered unseemly. That's right, white slaves. Until further legislation in 1826, Whites were enslaved as well. People preferred to call it 'indentured', but, at the end of the day, it was all the same. Naturally enough, white slaves were drawn from poor families, commonly referred to as poor white trash. Quite often parents would have to sell off a couple of their own children to amass enough money to hold the rest of the family together for a while. Without doubt, the most famous slave in American history is Andrew Johnson who became President after

Lincoln was assassinated which does, you will admit, have a nice irony about it. In his youth he had absconded and been posted as a runaway with a reward for his return.

ONLY COFFEE CONTAINS CAFFEINE

It is doubtless the substance's name and the fact that it is mainly coffee that advertises itself as decaffeinated, that has caused people to link the drug exclusively with coffee. Tea contains almost identical quantities of caffeine, about 50mg per cup, and it is also present in chocolate and cola-type drinks.

Nor is there any firm evidence that there is a link between caffeine and heart disease; instead it would appear that the type of person who tends to consume large quantities of coffee is prone to heart conditions because of other facets of their lifestyle. Actually, scientists are worried about the decaffeinated brands since solvents, such as trichlorethylene, used in the extraction process leave traces in the product.

OWLS – THEIR VISUAL CAPABILITIES AND SAGACITY

Owls are generally regarded as having extremely limited day vision, supposedly the price that Mother Nature extracted in payment for the blessing of their excellent night vision. Actually, the bird's day vision is much better than man's; the main reason they hunt at night being that the small rodents upon which they prey are more active at such times.

The origin of the owl as a symbol of wisdom seems to date from ancient Greece, but the motive behind the choice of bird is obscure. As a matter of fact, owls are pretty stupid, even by bird-brain standards.

OXTAIL SOUP CONTAINS OXTAILS

Actually it contains ordinary cow's tails, but the manufacturers evidently don't think that this sounds appetising enough.

OYSTERS AND THE 'R' IN THE MONTH

Many people still believe that for some reason oysters become poisonous between 1 May and 31 August. Fortunately, there being no calendars at the bottom of the sea, the oysters themselves remain blissfully unaware of the changing months and annually neglect to turn toxic. Around May and June, when the sea temperature climbs to about 80° F, the oysters release their sex cells into the water and, during this mating season, they may contain less glycogen and tend to be a little paler, but are certainly not poisonous. In the days before refrigeration, it would have been dangerous to keep any seafood for that extra day or two and shellfish are the most dangerous in this respect, especially in the hot months which, by coincidence, have no 'R's in them. The reason that the belief became specifically attached to the oyster is that they were once the commonest and cheapest of all the shellfish available. Dr Johnson is recorded as feeding his cat on them, and always made a point of going to the shops for them himself to save his manservant the indignity of being seen purchasing them.

Needless to say, there is no aphrodisiac effect produced by eating oysters; containing less than ten calories apiece, they are a remarkably poor source of energy of any sort. A diet of oysters would soon leave any apsiring bedroom athlete too weak to raise the shells of his next meal, let alone anything else!

P

PACHYDERMS ARE ELEPHANTS

A goodly number of people would confidently bet that
'pachyderm' is merely a synonym for 'elephant' – they
would lose! Deriving from the Greek *pakhudermos* –
meaning thick-skinned, the term applies to any hoofed
or ungulate quadruped which does not chew the cud.
This would include horses and pigs, as well as
elephants, rhinos and hippos. In other words, all
elephants are pachyderms, but not all pachyderms are
elephants.

THE PACIFIC OCEAN WAS DISCOVERED BY CORTEZ

Nine out of ten people would tell you that the above is
true, but they would only be perpetuating a myth that
has been going on for years. Perhaps the best known
example of the mistake being enshrined in literature is
the following extract from the well-known sonnet by
Keats.

> Then I felt like some watcher of the skies
> When a new planet swims into his ken,
> Or like stout Cortez when, with eagle eyes,
> He stared at the Pacific – and all his men
> Looked at each other with a wild surmise –
> Silent, upon a peak in Darien.

Look through any art book and you will find reproductions of paintings depicting amazed Spaniards gazing at
the Pacific, the central character being referred to as
Cortez, but he is in fact Vasco Nunez de Balboa.

In 1520, Balboa joined Fernandez de Encisco's
expedition bound for the Gulf of Urba. This move was

not really prompted by the call of the great unknown, but from a pressing need to escape an ever-increasing battalion of creditors – he was compelled to join the ship hidden inside a barrel! Nevertheless he soon took command of the expedition, sending its deposed leader back to Spain in chains. Encouraged by tales from the Indians of a great sea on the other side of the Isthmus of Panama, he pushed on until, on 25 September 1513, he first sighted the Pacific from the aforementioned peak in Darien. On the same day he despatched a scouting party which included Francisco Pizzaro and Alonzo Martin, and it was this group who first stood on the shores, Balboa not arriving to join them until the 29th. Nor was he the first European to sail upon the waters, that already having been done by Martin in a small boat on the Gulf of St Michael.

Although they discovered it, members of this expedition did not, however, name the ocean. This was done by Magellan in 1520 who was grateful for the calm waters after his less than tranquil passage through the Straits of Magellan.

'PEACE IN OUR TIME'

In the Book of Common Prayer, the words 'Give peace in our time, O Lord' do appear, but what Chamberlain spoke of was 'Peace for our time'. Nor was he a silly old duffer bamboozled by Hitler and his entourage of psychopaths. A few days after his having used these words to the public, he was warning the Commons not to place much hope on comments that he had made 'in a moment of some emotion, after a long and exhausting day' – not that this means that the man was necessarily 'tired and emotional' in the now accepted sense of the expression.

PEACOCK'S TAIL FEATHERS

Those which are commonly referred to as the tail feathers are actually growing on the creature's back. The peacock's tail comprises no more than twenty or so feathers all of which are dull, brown and uninteresting.

PEOPLE MISSING FOR SEVEN YEARS CAN BE DECLARED DEAD

Just because *you* haven't seen someone for seven years does not entitle you to have them declared 'legally' dead; it might be that they just didn't want to see you for seven years. Even if they have apparently disappeared into thin air leaving possessions and active bank accounts, death cannot simply be assumed and automatically granted legal status after any period of time. While talking about people missing for protracted periods, it is worth mentioning that the old tear-jerkers telling of a soldier, or whoever, suffering from global amnesia only to recover his memory to find himself legally dead and his wife remarried, are just that, tear-jerkers. There are no authenticated cases of such melodramas.

PEOPLE SUFFERING FROM A COLD EXPERIENCE A REDUCTION IN TASTE CAPABILITY

The five taste functions – acid, alkaline, sweet, bitter and saline – remain at normal efficiency during the most virulent of colds. It is the sense of smell that all but disappears. The nasal congestion restricts the normal movement of air from the mouth to the nose, thus preventing the olfactory senses augmenting those of taste, as they usually do. Any person who is blindfolded and fitted with a nose peg, has extreme difficulty in distinguishing between various foodstuffs.

ST PETER'S IS THE MAIN CATHOLIC CHURCH IN ROME, AND THE WORLD

It is certainly the most famous and most publicised, but it is not the main one. That honour goes to the relatively unheard of St Giovanni in Laterano (St John Lateran), which is officially the Cathedral of Rome and Metropolitan Church of its Bishops. The building also bears the inscription 'Mother And Head Of All Churches In The City And The World'.

PHILOMELA AS A ROMANTIC NAME FOR A NIGHTINGALE

The poetic name for a nightingale is based on a confusion surrounding an incident in Greek mythology which has caught out many a poet of note. The myth concerns Tereus, the King of Thrace who, although married to Procne, raped her sister Philomela, and then cut out her tongue and imprisoned her to prevent the story leaking back to his wife. Eventually Procne found out and, in a blind rage, killed her own son, Itys, and served up bits of him to her husband, later telling him what she had done. The news transfixed him to the spot allowing the sisters to make their escape, but he later caught up with them and was on the point of killing them when the gods intervened and changed *Procne* into a nightingale, Philomela they changed into a swallow since her tongue had been cut out, the swallow never actually singing, only twittering. Poets perhaps chose to confuse the two, Philomela being far more lyrical than Procne with which nothing would appear to rhyme.

Another mistake made by writers of all sorts throughout the ages, is to refer to the sweet-singing bird as 'she'. Only the male of the species ever sings!

THE PILGRIM FATHERS FOUNDED THE FIRST SETTLEMENT IN THE NEW WORLD

The settlers who landed in America, in 1620, were called many things ranging from 'The Scrooby Group', because they mainly came from Scrooby in Nottinghamshire, to the less than complimentary 'puke-stockings', which was resentfully applied by the *Mayflower*'s crew who had the misfortune to be preached at and remonstrated with about their nasty crude ways all across the Atlantic by their sanctimonious cargo. They were never called the Pilgrim Fathers for the very simple reason that that term did not emerge until the opening of the nineteenth century.

As for them being the first settlers with their camp at Plymouth, this just isn't so. Thirteen years before in 1607, Sir John Popham, Chief Justice of England, funded the founding of a colony led by his brother George. One hundred and twenty people journeyed with Popham to settle at the mouth of the Kennebec river in what is now Maine. But a few months after, George Popham died and shortly after that his second-in-command, Raleigh Gilbert, returned to England to assume a large family fortune. These two events, which left the colony without leadership and short of supplies, led to the rapid disintegration of the settlement which was abandoned in 1608, but this can in no way detract from the fact that it was the first settlement of Europeans in America.

THE PONY EXPRESS

Still we have the 'derring-do' image of the valiant Pony ('The mail must get through') Express rider arriving at the fort, riddled with arrows, just to deliver the message that there ain't no mail, before expiring in the saddle. Unfortunately, it was hardly like that. The venture was a complete and utter disaster, which was mainly due to the calibre of man that the job attracted. The company only survived a very rocky year and a half before disappearing into the wild blue yonder – just as its riders had tended to do when they got bored or encountered hostile Indians.

PORCUPINES AND THEIR QUILLS

Porcupines cannot 'fire' their quills at aggressors; they do lash out with their tails causing some quills to fall out, but this is hardly the same thing. In the past, there was a lot of 'evidence' to support the 'firing' theory. When people shot large game and found several quills embedded to a considerable depth in the carcass, it was naturally decided that they had been shot in like missiles.

Once an animal has picked up a few quills as the result of an unwisely intimate contact with one of these bizarre little creatures, the moisture and warmth of the host's body cause barbs to swell up at the quill tip. In many anatomical locations, extraction is impossible for non-dactyl animals, and any muscular activity at the injury site only causes the spines to work their way inwards. In many cases, this has caused the death of animals as big as bears and, given a hunter who finds a dead bear with no other injuries save some porcupine quills embedded up to the hilt, it is not hard to see how the notion got going.

Finally, female porcupines do not always die in labour due to internal damage done to them by the spines of the litter. At birth the animal only has what can best be described as its 'milk' quills. These are short, soft, white and quite pliable.

PORTHOLES IN SHIPS

It would be quite remarkable if modern liners were fitted with portholes, since that term only refers to the traps through which cannon were fired in the days of Nelson, etc. A ship's cabin window is called a scuttle.

PORTLAND CEMENT AND THE ISLE OF PORTLAND

There is no physical connection between the cement and the isle – the former has never been manufactured in the latter. The cement's colour so resembled that of Portland stone that the name was applied. Neither is the Isle of Portland an island; it is a peninsular.

'POSH' DERIVED FROM 'PORT OUT, STARBOARD HOME'

The statement in the heading must be the most widely held misconception in the field of word and phrase origins. The story goes that, in the days of British India, the upper crust, travelling to that bastion of the Empire, always booked a portside cabin for the outward journey, and a starboard one for the return. The purpose of so booking with P & O, was to ensure a shaded cabin for both legs of the trips. Although this seems to be a beautifully neat explanation, it is unfortunately false, for the P & O booking records go back to 1849 and they cannot find any evidence of a single 'posh' booking. In addition to this, contact with Mr S. Rabson, the P & O company librarian, reveals that the side of the ship in relation to its direction was irrelevant to the price of the cabins – so where are the connotations of wealth and prestige? Nor would there be any comfort advantage to so booking. Your cabin would be in the sun all morning for the majority of the trip – until they opened the Suez Canal, that is. After midday, when the heat rose dramatically, it would be all but irrelevant where your cabin was located. Besides, who stayed in their cabins all day? Another point is that just as many people made the trip in reverse. So what happened to 'soph' – a natural development, one would have thought, given the word 'sophisticated'.

The OED records the first appearance of the word as being in 1918 as a term for a dandy, but cites no seafaring connections. The real origin will doubtless remain obscure.

POWDERED GLASS IN FOOD CAN KILL PEOPLE

Countless must be the novels, films and plays that have nurtured this myth into old age. Glass is not a poison and, if ground up into such a fine powder as to be undetectable in the mouth, it will simply pass through the system doing no harm whatsoever. And that particle size would have to be very small, as anyone who has eaten a sandwich containing but a few grains of fine sand can testify. If, on the other hand, the glass were broken into pieces large and irregular enough to cause severe and terminal internal injury, who but an idiot would or could sit chewing the first mouthful?

PREGNANT WOMEN AND FALLS

One of the stock scenes of romantic tragedy and soap operas is that of the pregnant heroine taking a tumble on the stairs – preferably long, sweeping, marble ones – and starting to miscarry within seconds of landing in an elegantly languid position at the bottom without a hair out of place or a blemish to the exquisitely made up face. Absolute rubbish! Babies are never as safe as when they are in the womb and are not going to be bothered in the slightest by such an incident – unless they are asleep and are rudely woken. A really heavy and protracted fall could cause some separation between the wall of the uterus and the placenta which would result in some bleeding, but not even this will cause the immediate onset of labour which, in films, always culminates in a stillborn child.

To stand any chance of bringing on labour by means of a fall, the mother would have to be heavily pregnant and taking a running swan-dive off the top step and land in a belly-flop at the bottom. Should any woman be sufficiently mad to do such a thing she could well burst her waters which would really start things moving, but, since she would have to be pretty well advanced to effect this, there is no reason why the baby should not be born alive and kicking. In effect, the only person likely to suffer injury or damage in a tumble on the stairs is the mother herself.

Another puzzling thing about silver screen pregnancies is that, as soon as delivery is imminent, everybody starts to charge around the place boiling horrendous quantities of water. What on earth for? What in the world are they going to do with it? The midwife who issues the orders for boiling water and organises everyone in the fruitless task of providing it never calls for any. There's nothing to sterilise; nobody's going to scrub-up in boiling water, and hopefully for the infant's sake, nobody is going to clean up the happy arrival with scalding water. Perhaps it is for a celebratory tea-party.

PRESS GANGS
Press gangs were not illegal kidnap gangs, they were invariably made up of existing naval personnel and operated with the full backing of the Crown and the law courts which, under the power of a widely effective Elizabethan Vagrancy Act, could direct numerous unfortunates to a life on the ocean waves. Nevertheless, it was not unknown for certain public-spirited, water-

front inn-keepers to mug a couple of their residents, having an arrangement with the local press gang to remove the victims. Nor was this gentle form of recruitment restricted to the navy, for the army had similar groups who worked the waterfronts and dock-lands alongside the navy until legislation at the end of the sixteenth century placed such areas off-limits to them. There was no humanitarian thinking behind this move, it was simply that the army enjoyed a higher rate of volunteers. Conditions for soldiers were infinitely better than those endured by sailors.

Strangely enough, the word 'press' does not have any link with 'force'; instead it stems from the now redundant 'prest money' – meaning 'lent money' deriv-ing from the French *preter* – to lend, the allusion being to the advance in wages given to each victim to seal his contract of 'enlistment'.

The reign of such gangs is not long over; the navy relying heavily upon their activities until well into the nineteenth century. If you are in the habit of frequenting the waterfronts and docklands, you are strongly advised to keep your weather eye out, for it is not yet illegal to press men into the navy, although an Act of 1835 stipulates that any man so forced must be released after five years of service. It's one way to see the world!

PRIDE GOETH BEFORE A FALL
A popular rendition of Proverbs 16: 18 – 'Pride goeth before destruction and an haughty spirit before a fall.'

THE PURITANS WERE A DOUR BUNCH WHO HABITUALLY DRESSED IN BLACK
Nobody could ever accuse the Puritans of being the wildest bunch of ravers that this country has ever seen, but they were nothing like the po-faced, hypocritical

kill-joys that history has unfairly painted them. They drank; they smoked; they were not violently 'anti-art'; Cromwell certainly patronised the arts and loved athletic games, music and fast horses, but did not go around with his head shaved à la Buddhist monk (see THE ROUNDHEADS ALL HAD SHAVEN HEADS). Nor did the Puritans habitually dress in black as an overstated badge of their austerity. Some may well have done so, but so too did a lot of non-Puritans; it was more of a social than a religious trait; people of all sorts of religious convictions continued to pall themselves in black for years after. You see, the name 'Puritan' was not a prissy accolade of self-professed sanctity carried by the individual, their collective intention was to purify the English Church of what they saw as the evil influence of Rome.

PYRAMIDS

The Great Pyramid at Giza may well be a massive structure, but it is a long way short of being the biggest pyramid of the ancient world. That distinction goes to Quetzalcoatl at Cholula de Rivadabia in Mexico, which exceeds the former by just under a million cubic yards.

For years, that ever present body of people who cannot rest until they have made a mystery out of the explicable or the mundane, have maintained the Pyramids to be everything from computers to shapes that concentrate the mystic powers of the universe, and that it was this cosmic force that preserved the mummies, not the embalming and bacteria free environment.

Tombs! That's what the Pyramids were – tombs! They were not complex calculating devices of mathematical or astronomic purpose. If they were, they weren't much use to anyone stuck out in the desert, miles away from anywhere. They did not produce mystical powers understood only by the ancient Egyptians; had that been the case, the shape would have featured everywhere in their culture.

The Pyramids were not built overnight – the Great Pyramid was some thirty odd years in construction with a permanent on-site labour force of 4,000. Every year, when the Nile was in full flood, this force was supplemented by a massive influx of over 100,000 agricultural workers who toiled for over three months. There were no unions, no 35½ hour week, no three weeks' holiday and non-contributory pension scheme; each man did two six-hour shifts every day of the week, with a long break over the hot midday.

A quick burst on your pocket calculator will reveal that this works out to just over 2,000 man hours for each of the 2,300,000 blocks brought from the specially built wharf and, with the use of ropes, log rollers and oxen, dragged up the ramp and manhandled into position. If you organised a gang of 100 Homo Armchairicus, provided them with similar equipment and told them that they had twenty hours to move one 2½-ton block of stone through similar distances, they could accomplish the task time and time again – especially if they knew that the penalty for failure was death.

Lastly we have the myth that was started in 1859 by John Taylor, a London based publisher, who stated that, after much 'study', he had discovered that the measurements and dimensions of the structures held the key to all the measurements and dimensions of the universe. Heady stuff indeed! Charles Smyth, Astronomer Royal for Scotland no less, took matters a great deal further by shooting off to Egypt and measuring everything in sight. He soon published his quite remarkable findings which, amongst other things, stated that if the area of the base of the Great Pyramid of Cheops was divided by the width of one of its own casing stones, the answer was 365 – the number of days in a year. Wow! Each casing stone being 25 inches wide was therefore equivalent to one ten-millionth of the Earth's radius as taken between the poles. Imagine! If you multiplied the height of the structure by various figures, the distance to the planets could be arrived at. Incredible! In short, the so-called 'findings' of Smyth and others of his type were nothing but a load of old Von Daniken.

The unkind might be tempted to think that it is possible to take any structure, or even a human being, and arrive at the desired distances by multiplying by 'various figures', but the jiggery-pokery went much further than that. As things turned out, the casing stones didn't really measure 25 inches – they were, in general, slightly bigger; a difficulty overcome by the dogged Smyth by inventing, right out of the blue, the sacred pyramid inch which managed to iron out any irksome irregularities. Some so-called 'pyramidologists' were actually found laboriously filing down casing stones of too rogue a size to be hammered into the great cosmic formula.

So, impressive, romantic, or whatever else the Pyramids might be to different people, there is no unfathomable mystery surrounding them per se, their purpose, or their much discussed construction which, in technical terms, is altogether less impressive than, for example, the very first suspension bridge, even taking the era difference into account. As for them being computers, this is just outlandish rubbish, and anyone who maintains that the Pyramids were astrological observatories and multipurpose and highly sophisticated cosmic calendars of space-age advancement is only demonstrating his total lack of knowledge of the level of ancient Egyptian astronomy. Their knowledge of the universe was virtually non-existent and they thought the world to be a rectangle with Egypt, naturally enough, slap-bang in the middle. Hardly super-advanced. The Pyramids are simply gargantuan monuments built to satisfy the overinflated egos of long-gone despotic megalomaniacs who thought that they were gods, wanted their place in eternity and who didn't give a damn how many people died in building it for them.

Just one last thing, the Pyramids are not the oldest stone-built monuments in the world; the megalithic chamber tombs of Western Europe pre-date them by several hundred years and were built without any help or influence from the so-called more civilised East of the day.

PYTHONS AND ANACONDAS CAN DEVOUR HUMAN BEINGS

The only thing about the constrictors that has not been grossly exaggerated is their unbelievable strength. If a fully grown python took it into its head to kill an ox, this it could do without so much as turning a scale; but why should it, it only kills that which it can eat whole and oxen hardly come into that category.

The upper size limit for both anacondas and pythons is something in the region of 30 feet, but those individuals that have approached this limit can legitimately be described as suffering from giantism, in that the norm is an average length of around 20 feet. Anacondas that grow to 30 feet have to stay in the water since they are no longer capable of efficient locomotion on land. Claims of anything between 40 feet and a ridiculous 200 feet persistently arise but such 'sightings' can be safely ignored. As the *Guinness Book of Animal Facts and Feats* puts it: 'Unfortunately many people forget that all animals must live within the laws of physics and chemistry.' The same passage points out that the internal organs remain uniform in size and therefore become progressively smaller and smaller in relation to increased body dimensions, there coming a point beyond which they simply cannot cope, and that point would arrive long before a body size of 40 feet, let alone 200 feet.

As for the idea of gargantuan serpents gulping down a couple of Bwanas for hors d'oeuvres, this can only happen in Tarzan movies. There have been a couple of authenticated cases when small children have met such a repugnant fate but, although these creatures could certainly kill a fully grown man, they could not possibly eat him. If the snake started swallowing at the head, then the shoulders would stick in the gullet, and if the snake attempted to eat its victim from the feet it would need the brains to manoeuvre both feet together to avoid a major problem in the middle of dinner. The python does not have such intellect.

Q

QUICKLIME WILL DESTROY CORPSES

Quicklime will not accelerate the decomposition of a human body – if anything it will act as a preservative!

Lime is extremely hygroscopic and needs moisture before it can generate any heat. The lime that surrounds the body will draw its water from that source producing a kind of mummification, which is the last thing that any murderer wants – as many have found out to their chagrin. Of further disadvantage is the fact that all the horrible little creatures of the soil that would otherwise speed the reduction of a corpse stay well clear of the location, being reluctant to chomp through a wall of quicklime to get at the body.

One of the earliest references to this fallacy is to be found in ancient Greece where they used to quarry limestone at Asos, in Lycia, for the construction of sarcophagi. The Greeks believed that such stone would eat up the body – that old fraud Pliny the Elder claimed to have conducted experiments and established beyond doubt that this was the case. It was as a result of this belief that such coffins gained their name, from *sarx* – 'flesh', and *phagein* – 'to eat'.

QUICKSAND DRAWS PEOPLE UNDER AND IS LETHAL

For a start, quicksand is not dry sand that is so fine of particle that one simply 'slides' through it. It is a water saturated area of sand that results not from a build-up of rainwater but from water rising from beneath under a very low pressure. In this suspended state, the grains of sand are quite frictionless and will support no weight at all, not in terms of a human or an animal standing on their feet, at any rate. Quicksand is, if you like, extremely sandy water.

Under no circumstances will quicksand suck people under to a horrible death. It is the victims themselves who generate any suction. Not unnaturally, anyone so caught immediately begins to struggle but, since it is a wet environment devoid of air, any attempt to extricate one foot will only cause downwards pressure on the other one.

Since quicksand is saturated sand it is, believe it or not, impossible to sink below its surface. It is far more buoyant than water so, unless you are carrying a pretty heavy sack, you will float at a line somewhere around your armpits. The only way to stand any chance of getting your head under the surface, if that's what you really want, is to raise your hands high above your head.

Although easy to say, calmness is your best weapon against quicksand. As soon as you realise your predicament divest any excess weight such as rucksacks, etc.; you will have plenty of time to do this, so don't panic. Next, irrational as it might sound, lie down flat on your back and, with the body weight so distributed, roll back to terra firma.

QUIVERS – POSITION OF IN MEDIEVAL DAYS

Perhaps it is because Hollywood produced many more films about Robin Hood, medieval conflict and knights of old, etc., that people imagine that the early archer carried his quiver on his back, Red Indian style. Douglas Fairbanks Jr might have done in his films of that genre, but the genuine article always slung his from his waist.

QUIZ

Most scholars prefer to believe that this word derived from 'inquisition', or an allied term, and scoff at the following.

A Dublin theatre manager named Daly took a bet that he could introduce a new word into the language within twenty-four hours. With the help of some no doubt inebriated aides, he chalked the word up all over the city centre, and in the morning everyone was asking what on earth 'quiz' was, so Daly won his bet. True it is a bizarre story, but not all respectable words have a respectable pedigree; not all have come to us from the classical languages, many have come from thieves' cant, slang, strip cartoons, mistaken translation and even from sheer sloppy speech. If 'quiz' did derive from 'inquisition', why did it wait until the end of the nineteenth century to put in an appearance? 'Inquisition' had been around for centuries by then. In addition to this, one of the earliest meanings of the word was hoax or a practical joke – far more in keeping with the antics of Mr Daly and friends than with those of Torquemada and Co.

R

RABBITS SHOULD BE LIFTED UP BY THEIR EARS

Anyone who really believes that any animal is happy being hauled up by its ears, should try being elevated likewise themselves. The rabbit's ears are of such proportions to enable it to hear well – not for man's convenience to pick the creature up. The proper way is to lift by the scruff of the neck whilst supporting the rump.

RAINING FISH

No book of 'unsolved mysteries' is complete without various 'authenticated' reports of torrential downpours of frogs, worms, and all sorts cascading from the heavens on to the heads of surprised people. Surprised! Half dead, more like! Being hit on the head by, shall we say, a 2-lb fish, for many of the reports have cited animals of this size, is not going to do anyone a great deal of good. Since fish are possessed of an aero-dynamically shaped body, they are going to have a terminal velocity of something in the region of 250 mph, and that would do more than ruffle your hair. Those same reports often claim that the fish are flapping about on the ground after landing which is surprising to say the least, for they are going to have more than a mild headache themselves.

Naturally enough, there have been attempts to update the myth with pseudo-scientific explanations of the phenomenon. The favourite story is that giant water-spouts are responsible. These supposedly pass over lakes and ponds sucking up all the fish who fall to earth when the waterspout collapses. Nice idea, but why is the waterspout so selective? Why hoover up just the fish?

What happens to all the twigs, algae, tin cans, old wellies, etc? Besides, no town could have a giant waterspout collapse on it and mistake the incident for a rainstorm.

ROBERT THE BRUCE WAS A SCOTSMAN
Alas for the Scots, to whom this man is a national hero, he was in fact French, his given name being Robert de Bruis. His family, of Norman nobility, landed with William the Conqueror.

ROLLS-ROYCE CARS
Apocrypha concerning these cars abound. The company has never maintained an 'our motor cars do not break down' policy and, at the drop of a title, despatched a battalion of bowler-hatted mechanics to the middle of the Sahara with a replacement back axle, and stoically refused payment because 'our motor cars etc . . .' They have gone to the ends of the earth to satisfy customers in the event of component failure, but that's another matter. Any lunatic who decides to drive his Rolls across the Afghan foothills and rips off his sump, will lose all his misconceptions about the company overnight.

Nor has the Spirit of Ecstasy ever been made out of silver, not by Rolls-Royce, at any rate. Initially it was cast in bronze and plated, but was later made of stainless steel. Nor was it always a fixture of the car. It was optional until 1920 when the craze of car mascots so distressed the company that they decided to create their own to prevent their radiators being desecrated by gold-gilt teddy bears, and the like.

ROMAN GALLEYS WERE MANNED BY CHAINED SLAVES WHO ROWED TO THE BEAT OF A DRUM

In eighteenth-century European galleys, convicts were condemned to row their lives away beside prisoners of war and the like, but this was rarely the case in the Roman navy; short-manned vessels would have drafted a few slaves and criminals but that was about the extent of the matter.

The popular image of the interior of a Roman galley, complete with hundreds of emaciated slaves pulling their hearts out to the beat of an enormous drum struck by a huge, stern-faced Nubian, is just nonsense straight out of Hollywood. For a start, mast and sail were used while under passage since even a crew in peak condition would have been hard pressed to row a galley much more than ten miles without collapsing; and they needed to conserve their strength for the considerable effort required to manoeuvre the vessel and wind the ship up to a maximum of about ten knots for ramming the enemy. The crew, sometimes as many as 200 in the case of a trireme, formed the greater part of a boarding party, so the Romans were hardly going to relish the prospect of unchaining, per vessel, 200 resentful slaves and felons who had nothing to lose but their chains by joining the enemy instead of fighting him. Since one could not really afford to have hundreds, possibly thousands, of men sitting idle during a naval engagement, for the most part, the Romans relied on free men for their oar power.

As for the huge, leopard skin clad Nubian time-keeper, he too is of modern imagination. Sharp sounding drums that could throw their note any distance at all did not emerge until the fourteenth century, and the dull, flat sound of the kind of drum that the Romans had covered with animal hide would not have been heard from one end of a rowing deck to the other – let alone through the other two decks. In battle, only the drummer himself would have been able to hear the beat which would have defeated the object somewhat. Most authorities seem to agree that high-pitched pipes or whistles were used since the higher the note, the higher the degree of penetration.

Simply for the sake of imparting the information, the last time that galleys were used in a warfare situation was in the Baltic, in 1809, during the Russo-Swedish War.

ROMANS USED CHARIOTS FOR WARFARE

They never did, not once. The Romans regarded their chariots as nothing more than instruments of transport or sport, and any possible military application did not fit in with their time-tested methods of warfare. Some countries did use them, but they were regarded with derision by most serious armies for, as a moment's thought will illustrate, a chariot is of little use without its horse-power, and a couple of well-placed arrows will soon remove that.

The Britons under Boadicea did use chariots in their final engagement with the Romans under Suetonius Paulinus, but they were not the fancy, well-made machines that you see in film 'reconstructions' of the era. They were cumbersome in the extreme, highly unmanoeuvrable, usually of a crude wicker construction and drawn, not by finely bedecked white chargers, but by pitifully expendable cart-horses.

Another favourite story about the chariots of old is that they were equipped with wicked-looking scythes attached to the wheel – as portrayed by the statue of Boadicea at Westminster Bridge, but again this is pure invention. There is no evidence that the chariots of any nation were ever fitted with such devices.

THE ROUNDHEADS ALL HAD SHAVEN HEADS

Despite the film industry engendered image, very few of the Parliamentary forces ever had short, cropped hair. The limited number who did follow the fad were typically the junior, overzealous types, who only did so to draw stark contrast between themselves and the rather more flamboyant Royalists, and to advertise the austerity of their characters. The craze soon fizzled out, and Lucy Hutchinson, a contemporary observer of events and detractor of Cromwell's wife, remarked that a few years after the war the use of the term would have caused some puzzlement. Cromwell himself had shoulder length hair, as did his sons and almost all his close associates and ministers.

RUGBY DEVELOPED AT RUGBY SCHOOL

Unfortunately for the alumni of that noble institution, the facts would appear to put this great British myth well and truly in the shade. Apart from anything else, there are records of a strikingly similar game having been played here since the Roman invasion; forms of football that permitted handling of the ball were nothing new in 1823, which was the year in which the originator of this myth sets his tale.

According to Matthew Bloxham, it was his fellow pupil William Webb Ellis who, in the middle of a perfectly ordinary game of football which was being played on 23 November 1823, suddenly and for no apparent reason, picked up the ball and ran down the pitch with it. Voila, rugby. It is indeed remarkable that Bloxham could be so accurate of date since the first time that he even bothered to mention this historic moment was in a letter to the school magazine nearly sixty years later.

One thing that makes Bloxham's yarn so unlikely is the public school mentality of the early nineteenth

century. Such institutions were very much ones of the
'Play up, play up and play the game' genre and a
flagrant breach of the rules such as picking up the ball
and running away with it would have been far more
likely to draw cries of 'Poor show!' and a good dubbing
in the dorm the same night, rather than shouts of 'What
a wheeze – let's play the game this way and call it Harry
ruggers.' Most significant of all is the fact that Ellis
himself died without ever having once mentioned the
incident, or even hinting that he had been in any way
responsible for the game's conception. There is not a
single piece of corroborative evidence for Bloxham's
flight of fancy, nor did any other boy at the school at the
time remember the game in question or any other similar
incident.

S

SAINTS ARE PORTRAYED WITH A HALO

The primitive custom of portraying important figures
with an all over body-glow or what we commonly call a
halo, has its roots deep in pagan culture and was merely
adopted by the Christian Church. Be that as it may, the
luminous glow adorning saints' heads is not a halo, it is
a nimbus. Ultimately deriving from the Greek word for a
threshing floor, most likely because of the circular path
trod by the oxen employed in the operation, 'halo' first
applied to the disc of the sun, the moon, or a shield, and
it still properly applies to the luminous glow to be seen
about either of those celestial bodies, but not saintly
ones.

SAMSON HAD HIS HAIR CUT BY DELILAH

If you want to be really pernickety, you could say that no one actually cut the man's hair, because the Bible says that his locks of hair were shaved off. Even so, this was not undertaken by Delilah but by a man whom she summoned after Samson had fallen asleep.

Another myth surrounding this character is that he confided the secret of his strength to Delilah because he was so besotted with her, but the book itself tells a different story! She badgered it out of Samson by constantly harassing him with questions or, as the Bible puts it in Judges 16: 16, 'And it came to pass, when she pressed him daily with her words, and urged him, so that his soul was vexed unto death; that he told her all his heart.'

SAP RISES

The notion about sap rising is presumably born of man's ideas about the direction of his own sexual drive, considering the usual phrases and innuendoes thus inspired. Sap actually moves from the centre of the tree trunk outwards towards the bark, so it travels through a horizontal, not a vertical, plane.

SARDINES ARE A TYPE OF FISH

The only way to define a sardine is to say that it is whatever fish is found in a tin marked 'Sardines'. There is no such fish! The term covers numerous breeds of small fish ranging from pilchards to herring and menhaden; the word originating from the fact that such fish abound along the shores of Sardinia.

SCALPING AS A RED INDIAN TRADITION

This particular myth has only gained such firm footing because the history of the New World was written by the Whites. The unpleasant truth of the matter is that it was the Dutch, British and French colonial governments who were responsible for all the wholesale hairlifting that went on. Before the arrival of the Whites it is *possible* that the Cree and Teton Dakotas took scalps, but many authorities doubt even that.

The Dutch seem to have started the revolting business of offering bounty for scalps in order to provide incentive for people to go and clear the indigenous population from land ripe for the stealing. The effectiveness of this little ploy was not lost on the British and French who offered bounty for the scalps of each other's settlers and respective Indian allies. Sometimes this grim trade could backfire in that both sides often ended up paying unscrupulous scalp-hunters for the hair of their own people. Eventually the practice became so widespread that everybody got in on the act. It became virtually impossible for army officers to stop their men scalping every dead Indian after an engagement and, outside the relatively civilised enclaves of the townships, any fallen foe, be he brown, white, black or red, stood a pretty good chance of contracting terminal alopecia. Scalps became a widely accepted instrument of trade amongst Whites; they were of a fixed and known value; they were impossible to forge; they were as good as gold in other words. They smelled a bit, but nothing's perfect. As late as the latter half of the nineteenth century, parts of the state of Arizona were still paying $250 for Apache scalps.

SCORPIONS COMMIT SUICIDE IF SURROUNDED BY FIRE

With the obvious exception of man, no animal ever commits suicide; and that includes the lemming (q.v.). Whether the product of a balanced mind or no, the decision to resort to suicide is just that, a decision, and a decision is the result of a thought process which is the privilege of man and man alone. Apart from anything else, the scorpion is incapable of stinging itself since the curvature of its sting is such that it may only be rendered operable when raised above the preabdomen and thrust forward. Having said that, it must be stated that it is also untrue that all poisonous animals are immune from their own venom; a scorpion can be killed by its own venom but, to be fair, it does require the administration of a dose in excess of 200 times the amount needed to kill a guinea pig. Armed with this knowledge, it becomes obvious that any scorpions killed in man-made battles, natural combat or mating, die as the result of brute force and puncture wounds, not poison.

Interestingly enough, there are large colonies of non-poisonous scorpions thriving in certain areas of Kent, having arrived in imports and subsequently wandered off. Although they are typically associated with hot climes, scorpions do not like the heat and are perfectly happy with the British weather.

'SCOT FREE' AS A SLUR ON THE SCOTS

The Scots have, deservedly some say, earned a wide reputation for being the slowest people in the world with a pound coin, but 'scot free' has nothing to do with them always avoiding their corner when it comes to getting the drinks in, or whatever. The word traces back to the Old Norse 'skot' meaning a contribution.

SCOTLAND YARD HAD POLICE CONNECTIONS

King Edgar, who ruled England from AD 959 to 975 presented Kenneth, King of Scotland, with a plot of land next to the Palace of Westminster, upon which he was to build a residence to be occupied by himself and his entourage when he made his annual visit to pay homage to the English Crown. With the succession to the throne of James I of England, who was also James VI of Scotland, the necessity for such a property disappeared. It was then divided into two to become Great Scotland Yard and Middle Scotland Yard, both being used as government offices.

It was the gentlemen of the press who were responsible for engendering the myth that there was a connection between the police force and Scotland Yard. In 1829, when Sir Robert Peel started the police as a recognised body, its offices were in Whitehall Place, which was near to, and accessible via, Scotland Yard. The latter was eagerly seized upon by the press who, after all, have never been renowned for their accuracy and attention to detail. Officialdom stubbornly clung to Whitehall Place as a title, but even they eventually had to concede and adopt the erroneous title, retaining it when the headquarters were moved to new premises.

ST SEBASTIAN WAS SHOT TO DEATH BY ARROWS

Although this is the way that virtually all artists depict the man's death, he was actually beaten to death. The Roman Emperor Diocletian ordered Sebastian's execution for his adoption of the Christian faith. After being left for dead by the archers Sebastian, former Captain of the Emperor's Pretorian Guard, was nursed back to health by Christians.

Once back on his feet, Sebastian took the rather short-sighted course of paying a visit to his former employer

145

to beg tolerance for all Christians. Not a man to make the same mistake twice, Diocletian had him beaten to death with clubs on the spot.

Rather ironically, he is the patron saint of archers and pin-makers!

SEQUOIA TREES ARE THE OLDEST LIVING THINGS ON EARTH

They are certainly the largest living things on the planet (the largest specimen, called General Sherman, measures over 100 feet in circumference at ground level), but the oldest they are not. Even at the grand old age of 3,000, General Sherman is a mere sapling compared to the 4,600-year-old bristlecone pine of California, where several other examples of 4,000 years plus have been found. Actually dendrochronologists project the potential life-span of a sequoia to be a maximum of 6,000 years, which is some 500 years more than the bristlecone. If this is true, then the sequoia could well yet wrest the longevity title from its diminutive rival, but this might not happen for many a year, or never.

There have been some unsubstantiated claims for Japanese cedars, placing them at over 7,000 years old. The totally ridiculous claims put forward for the Canary Island dragon tree (some in excess of 10,000 years) must be discarded until enthusiasm is replaced by hard evidence.

SHARKS – MYTHS SURROUNDING

Most persistent of the myths connected with sharks is that they never sleep. The justification put forward for this is that, since the animal has no gills to pump water, it must therefore continually move through the sea to generate water circulation and respiration. It may be true that the shark has no gills, but they can use their mouths as a kind of suction pump to draw water in and out of the gill slits, and find no difficulty in continuing this function after dozing off. It is mackerel and tuna who are the condemned insomniacs.

Another fallacious idea is that the shark must roll over on to its side or its back to take a bite out of something, since the location of its jaw precludes a frontal attack. For a head-on bite, the bottom jaw moves forwards, the snout is raised high and both sets of teeth cantilever forwards enabling the shark to take as many frontal bites as he chooses.

Nor is the shark poorly sighted – quite the contrary! The physical make-up of a shark's eye is very similar to that of a cat, in that the construction includes a tapetum which is a reflective layer located behind the retina. When an image is received by the eye, the tapetum causes it to be fired back through the optic rods a second time, thus allowing the shark a 'double take' at everything it sees. Equipped with this system the fish sees only too well, even in very poor light. If the shark needs to surface in bright sunlight, there is an automatic filter that comes into play to prevent temporary blindness. No, there is nothing wrong with a shark's eyesight!

THOMAS SHERATON MADE FURNITURE

Sheraton produced designs not furniture – that he left to others. There is in existence one glass-fronted bookcase which bears the initials 'T.S.' in one of the drawers, but not everybody accepts that the piece was made by Sheraton himself. To all intents and purposes, it is probably fair to say that the man never made so much as a stick of furniture in his life. In fact, the term 'Sheraton' has no real meaning in the antique world, it being nothing more than a rough indication of the style and flavour of a piece, possibly of its period, but certainly not of its maker.

By all accounts something of a rather ephemeral weirdo, Sheraton arrived in London some time around 1790 and became a shopkeeper, author and designer. There is no record whatsoever of him ever having a workshop. The only thing that he was any good at was furniture designing, but not even that was enough to save him from a pauper's death in 1860.

SINGAPORE FELL BECAUSE ALL THE GUNS POINTED THE WRONG WAY

How this completely fallacious story got going is not known, but get going it most certainly did, being given credence by no less a man than Winston Churchill who should have known better, but, there again, perhaps he did! The question as to why the myth grew up is altogether easier to answer.

The fall of Singapore was a significant and heartfelt blow to this country, and if a silly reason for it could be found, like all the guns being fixed pointing seaward and the unsporting Japanese creeping out of the jungle behind, then it turned a monumental defeat into a silly and cruel trick of fate; something which is always easier to bear. The facts of the matter are that the defensive guns not only could come to bear on the invaders, but that some artillery units were pouring shells on to the Japanese for three days without a pause. The majority of the guns could pan through 360°; the only ones incapable of this being land-mounted naval guns whose arcs were dictated by the stops on their mounting plates.

SKIN DOES OR NEEDS TO BREATHE

The most famous example of the film industry's efforts to perpetuate this myth occurs in the first part of 'Goldfinger'. James Bond finds a beautiful girl who is very naked and very dead. As far as the film is concerned, the cause of death is her having been completely covered with gold paint and suffocated as a rapid result. This may look good for the camera, but that's about as far as it goes.

Frogs may breathe through their skin, but man does not! The human skin does not 'inhale' in any way and it is only responsible for the discharge of something less than 1/200th of the total carbon dioxide. Any cosmetics manufacturer who claims that his products enable or allow the skin to breathe ought to be liable for prosecution under the Trades Descriptions Act, since neither the skin nor the pores breathe under any circumstances. If they did, people who spend hours under water Schnorkeling would be in a great deal of trouble.

THE SLEEPING BEAUTY WAS WOKEN WITH A KISS

Before the tale was bowdlerised to make it suitable for the tender ears of more recent generations, the attentions that the fair maid received to arouse her from her slumber were of a somewhat more intimate and protracted nature than a quick peck on the cheek. The fact that the naughty knight tarried not to take off all his armour was also said to have helped to wrest the girl from the arms of Morpheus.

SLIPPED DISCS

Due to the somewhat inappropriate term for the condition, the popular mind imagines it to be quite literally a section of the spine that has slipped out of line. Interspersed with the vertebrae are fibro-cartilaginous sections that act as shock-absorbers and, under certain conditions, these spacers can prolapse and put pressure on the spine. Surgery is rarely needed, yet in extreme cases injections of chymopapain, an enzyme derived from the paw-paw, are administered to dissolve the instrusive section.

SMOKE FROM BROWN PAPER STUPEFIES BEES
There is no quirk in the bee's respiratory system that renders it insensible by the simple method of burning brown paper. The smoke only alarms the bee which, in such a state, immediately begins to fill its honey sacs from the hive's foodstore to make ready for any contingency. Obsessed with this prime task, the inhabitants of the hive remain oblivious to careful human interference in the dwelling.

SNAKES ARE DEAF AND CAN BE CHARMED
First, let us get rid of the old idea that, having no visible ears, snakes are therefore deaf to airborne sound and can only receive vibration through the ground. Snakes do have ears, not like those of other creatures perhaps, but ears nevertheless. Beneath the surface of the face, covered by skin and muscle, lies a thin bone plate called the quadrate bone. It was once part of the skull but is now detached and is held in place by ligaments to act as a pressure plate for sound. The columella attached to the inside surface of the quadrate bone conducts vibrations to the expanded inner ear which lies in the oval window of the cochlea. Obviously snakes are better suited than most creatures to picking up vibrations in the ground, but many other animals, including human beings, are quite capable of doing so as well, albeit to a lesser degree.

Despite the fact that some birds and small rodents can become transfixed with fear in the presence of a snake, the snake has no hypnotic powers to charm prey into its reach. Nor, on the other hand, can it be hypnotised by the 'snake charmer's' flute for the very simple reason that the animal cannot hear it. The snake's hearing range is all in the low frequency band, between 100 and 700 hertz, which is far below that of the flute. The creature responds to two things; the tapping of the charmer's foot, and the side to side motion of the flute which the snake appears to emulate. But, the swaying motion of the snake is nothing more than a physical necessity for, without the motion, the snake is incapable of remaining erect; and erect it wants to remain because it is trying to estimate the distance between itself and the charmer in case it needs to strike. A prerequisite for a long and healthy career in the snake-charming business is the ability to make very accurate assessments of a snake's striking range (usually two-thirds of its body length) and to remain in motion just beyond reach – although not so far beyond that your partner loses interest and ceases to perform. If a forgetful charmer should cease swaying around long enough for his partner to get a fix on him, then the snake could find itself going solo!

Lastly, snakes cannot die from swallowing their own venom, nor in fact can any other animal, humans included, since the venom is merely a modified form of enzyme or saliva, and is only toxic if introduced into the bloodstream. The same is true of curare, the South American poison which, though lethal when applied to the tips of arrows, has found a place in modern anaesthetics. It is said to taste something like honey and can be eaten by the spoonful.

SNOB

This term is rarely, if ever, applied to the people who conform to the dictionary definition of a snob. A snob is not an arrogant type of high social standing who looks down his nose at those he considers to be beneath him –

he is exactly the opposite. To quote the OED, a snob is: 'A person belonging to the lower classes of society, one having no pretensions to rank or quality', or, 'A vulgar or ostentatious person'. To put it bluntly, a snob is a lower class crawler to the upper classes. Because of this, one of the word's earliest applications was to serve as a nickname for cobblers; this was meant to be a pun on the fact that a man in such a trade spent his life looking up to his customers.

The term developed from the early days of Oxford and Cambridge where new students not only had to register their names but also their ranks; those of noble birth being obliged to log their title, and those not so elevated of station being obliged to put *sine nobilitate* – the Latin for 'without nobility'. This was later abbreviated to 's. nob.' and the word coined by the titled members of the universities to describe those untitled students who kept trying to mix with the 'nobs' and ingratiate themselves with their betters.

SPINACH IS A PRIME SOURCE OF IRON
With all due respect to the plant and Popeye, it is no such thing.

In 1870, a government department published a table giving the nutritional value of most foods. Either as a result of a mistake in the figures or of a simple typographical error, the decimal point in the figure giving the iron content of spinach was misplaced one step to the right, thus giving everyone the idea that spinach had ten times more iron than any other green vegetable, whereas it holds pretty much the same.

SPONTANEOUS COMBUSTION OF HUMAN BEINGS

The human body is non-combustible. It is nearly 70 per cent water and can no more burst into flames than can meat in a butcher's shop. People's clothing has suddenly and for no *immediately* apparent reason gone up in flames with fatal results, but nobody's body has ever exploded. It is perfectly possible that the mystery cause is nothing more sinister than a cigarette burn that smoulders unnoticed for a time before being caught by a freak draught, or someone nearby striking a match, the head of which flies off on to a nylon dress, and the striker being unwilling to proffer such information after the tragic consequences. People have not altered structurally in the past few thousand years, yet it is only as recently as the widespread use of synthetic fibres that many such stories started circulating. Watching someone remove a nylon dress in the dark can be quite illuminating; there are sparks all over the place. Perhaps, under the right circumstances (a little spilt alcohol at a party could well be enough), a nylon dress rubbing against a nylon shirt could spark itself off – but never its wearer.

DR SPOONER KEPT MAKING 'SPOONERISMS'

There is no need to dwell on the many spoonerisms attributed to Dr Spooner, one time Warden of New College, Oxford. Better to leave it to the words of the man himself, as taken from an interview with the London *Evening Standard* of 22 July 1924, when Spooner would have been in his eightieth year.

'I suppose you really want to know the latest Spoonerism? Well, it might interest you to know that I don't think that I have ever intentionally made a Spoonerism in my life, and in fact, I don't remember ever having made one. I know that it is very sad to destroy the illusions of England in this way, but this is a thing that is true.'

'STAND ON CEREMONY' MEANS TO BEHAVE FORMALLY

This is a much misused expression that actually means to believe in forecasts and prophecies, not the observance of protocol.

In Shakespeare's *Julius Caesar* Act II, Scene 2, Caesar is being warned not to venture out on the Ides of March since all the signs and portents are bad. Calpurnia, his wife, says: 'Caesar, I never stood on ceremony, yet now they fright me' – meaning that, although she never believed in portents before, they did worry her then.

THE STORMING OF THE WINTER PALACE

As with the storming of the Bastille, the so-called storming of the Winter Palace was far more important in its symbolism to the people than it was in any military or practical sense. This has never stopped the Russians from fostering the image of the noble, proud, peasant army dying in great numbers as it marched resolutely towards its destiny and the taking of the Winter Palace to silence forever the death rattle of the filthy Tsarist regime. Every other nation hams up its symbolic fiascos, so why shouldn't the Russians?

As you will no doubt have gathered from the tone so far, there was no last ditch shoot-out between the Bolsheviks and Kerensky's government and the massive, brooding canvases showing such are a complete distortion of the facts. If anything, the night of 7 November 1917 belongs to the world of farce.

Things began to hot up a little when the Bolsheviks grew tired of sitting around wondering what to do next and sent an ultimatum to Kerensky at the palace. By the time someone had been found to deliver the message, and he in turn had made his way there on a bicycle, there was only about five minutes of the allowed time left to run. Since the note told Kerensky that the guns of the cruiser *Aurora* and those of the Fortress of Peter and Paul were trained on the palace and that they would open up before any infantry attack, Kerensky decided, quite sensibly, that he had had a bellyful of politics anyway. He told the palace's 'defenders' (a small detachment of cadets and a women's battalion) that the game had been played and that they had best make themselves scarce.

Clasping Kerensky's acceptance of the terms of the ultimatum in his hot little hand, the messenger leapt astride his trusty steed once more and began to peddle back to his own HQ. He never made it in time. Unwitting of the time that it had taken their messenger to complete his mission, the revolutionaries assumed the absence of a reply to be a curt refusal of their terms and decided to send out the prearranged signal to the guns to open fire. The only trouble was that the signal involved a red lantern and no one could find one. When they did, the signal was made and the sky lit by a fearful barrage as the ship and the fort popped off round after round – of blanks, the only ammunition they had. Undeterred, the Bolsheviks marched on the Winter Palace and there was some sporadic gunfire around the grounds which resulted in the deaths of six of the invaders, shot by their own side in all the confusion. At a loss for anything more constructive to do, Kerensky simply wandered out of his office, got into his car and drove away leaving the Bolsheviks hopelessly lost in the labyrinth of the palace's 2,000-odd rooms.

STRAITJACKET

The above is the proper spelling and there is no connection with the word 'straight', although the jacket does have the effect of holding the wearer so. The source is the Old English *streit* – meaning narrow or tight, a word still extant in expressions like 'strait-laced' or 'straitened circumstances'; not to mention 'straits' as applied to a narrow stretch of water.

SURVIVAL OF THE FITTEST MEANS THE SUPERIORITY OF GIVEN SPECIES

When Herbert Spencer coined this phrase he did not attach to it any connotation of superiority. Quite the contrary! He employed the term 'fittest' in the sense of 'best suited to survive'; this applied whether the creatures were strong or weak and stupid.

As stated, it was Spencer who coined the expression, not Darwin. Wells and Huxley also expounded upon the theme that Darwin initially preferred to call 'natural selection', but it was only the latter who became the target of unfounded invective from religious fundamentalists, who had evidently not taken the trouble to read the work that they were damning.

THE SWALLOWS OF CAPISTRANO MIGRATE AND RETURN EN MASSE

Anyone journeying to the mission of San Juan at Capistrano, California, on 19 March, in the hope of seeing enormous clouds of returning swallows, is going to be disappointed – no matter what the song says! Conversely, there is no mass departure on 23 October, the anniversary of the death of San Juan. It must be said that this has never stopped thousands of people turning up at this location every year, and doubtless never will.

SWANS CAN BREAK A MAN'S ARM WITH THEIR WINGS AND SING BEFORE DYING

The notion that an angry swan can break arms and legs in frenzied attacks on man belongs to the realm of myth. If the bones in a swan's wing were of sufficient thickness and density to come off better in a collision with a human arm, then the bird would never be able to get off the ground. Like geese, swans are pretty intimidatory when riled and one would be well advised to retreat, but the ferocity, frequency and overall effectiveness of attacks on humans are greatly exaggerated.

As for the romantic idea that these birds sing but once in their lives and then only before dying, this may have given us the expression 'swan song', as used to describe someone's last performance or act, but this too is nothing but folklore. No swan ever sings; they honk and hiss, but are quite incapable of anything more melodious.

There is another myth attached to these regal birds — that they are all the property of the crown. At an annual event called swan-upping, all new birds are trapped and marked according to their owners. Those of the crown are given five nicks in the beak, and those belonging to the various trade's companies and corporations, a varying number of nicks. Birds that are the property of, for example, the Dyers' and Vintners' Company, receive two nicks in the beak, hence the popular pub sign 'The Swan with Two Necks', which is a corruption of 'the swan with two nicks'.

SWEDEN HAS THE HIGHEST SUICIDE RATE

It is often understandable how some myths originate. You can find a reason why the truth becomes twisted along the way, but, in the case of the above, the reason for the myth's beginning is as obscure as the myth itself is longstanding. Perhaps it was assumed that a race that had apparently little else to do except watch Ingmar Bergman films and flood the rest of the planet with porno magazines, would find death a blessed release.

To put the record straight, it is Hungary that leads the field with a suicide rate of 42.6 per 1,000 head of population; and there are several others, including the gentle Swiss, who come before Sweden. Jordan has the claim to the lowest rate, which is an intriguing .04 per 1,000. Quite how .04 of a person contrives to rush rudely unannounced into the presence of their creator is a point to ponder, but that's what the statistics say.

SYPHILIS IS ONLY TRANSMITTED THROUGH SEXUAL INTERCOURSE

As some have found out to their dismay, and the doubtless disbelief of their partner, this just isn't so. It is probably the destruction of the old 'lavatory seat' bogey that has caused the pendulum to swing too far the other way. One of the more bizarre cases of an 'innocent' party contracting the disease, is that of someone whose hand was grazed by the teeth of an infected man who was playing in the same football match! Kissing can quite easily be sufficient contact to ensure contamination, and an accidental contact between a broken skin site and a sore on an infected person can do the job just as well. Cups, spoons, towels and sheets used by an infected individual have also been known to transfer the disease. Fortunately, such articles retain their ability to infect for a short time only but, dare it be said, when, for example, taking Holy Communion, you don't always know the person before you in the line for the wine!

SYPHILIS WAS A PRESENT FROM THE RED INDIANS

The White man may have murdered, raped and cheated the Red Indian out of everything that he ever owned, including his pride, but, according to myth, the chiefs can rest peacefully in the Happy Hunting Grounds because they gave the White man syphilis in exchange. It seems to be the notion that this condition was unknown until Columbus and his crew returned from the New World, having become overfriendly with the natives and picked up the local culture, so to speak. Unfortunately, it is necessary to rob the Indian of even this Parthian pleasure, for John O'Gaunt is known to have died of a malignant disease of the genitals in 1408 (Columbus not returning until 1493) and it is almost certain that Herod went the same way. There is no freak peculiarity in the genital structure of the American Indian to make him alone the harbinger of this ill; sexual diseases have been around almost as long as sex itself.

Syphilis did not get its name until 1530, thirty-seven years after Columbus returned which, in terms of history, is only the next day, so perhaps later medico-historians simply linked the two events, added two and two together and came up with five. People have been dying of syphilis for thousands of years, they just didn't know what to call it. Syphilis is notoriously protean in its manifestation, and it is generally accepted today that in ancient times syphilis would have been confused with leprosy (q.v.) and tuberculosis. People have also been dying of the disease until surprisingly recently. Al Capone degenerated to death with it, and our own Winston Churchill's father died of the condition. Contrary to popular belief, Hitler was not afflicted (see under HITLER).

The term itself derives from a poem written in 1530 by Girolamo Fracastoro, an Italian poet and physician of Verona. The work was entitled, 'Syphilis, or the

French Disease' – the second part of the title being one of the names the condition had gone by some time before due to an outbreak of the condition of epidemic proportions amongst the French soldiers occupied in the siege of Naples in 1494. Syphilis was the name of the 'hero' of the piece; he curses the sun during a heatwave and is given the disease as punishment for his folly. His name means lover of pigs – he was a swineherd by trade.

T

TABLE FORKS
Despite the modern penchant for portraying Tudor banquets as affairs of great gluttony, with bones being tossed to waiting hounds and greasy fingers being wiped on the diner's chest, table forks were around for a long time before Henry VIII was even born. They were in common use amongst the higher echelons of society and were usually of precious metals and finely worked. There are several examples of their being willed as heirlooms in pre-Tudor documents.

TAPEWORMS IN MAN
Revolting as these creatures are, the invaded human host is invariably ignorant of their presence. Morbid and chronic hunger is not a typical indication of their invasion since they do not lie in the gut gorging themselves on food ingested by the host. Even though they can exceed some 30 feet in length, they never cause intestinal blockage.

TARANTULAS AND THE TARENTELLA

There seems to be a great deal of confusion about the relationship between the name of the spider and that of the dance, the tarentella. The most popular story is that the dance developed as a means of neutralising the spider's venom, which would only happen after it had passed the heart once. The wilder the dance, the quicker the bloodflow, and the greater the chance of survival. The truth is that neither the spider nor the dance is named for each other; they are both independently named after Taranto, in Italy, where the spider abounded, and a kind of wild hysteria regularly beset the locals, resulting in some pretty peculiar behaviour that became known as tarantism.

For many centuries, from the Middle Ages onwards in fact, reports of whole towns or areas breaking out in mass hysteria were common throughout Europe. The cause was not spiritual invasion, as was then commonly believed and still held by some, nor was it spider bites; it was ergot poisoning. This resulted from people eating bread made from diseased rye which produced a condition not unlike St Anthony's Fire. Hallucinations (ergot is a source of LSD), muscular spasm and delirium were typical symptoms. As a direct result of the prevalence of such behaviour, composers began writing lively dance pieces called tarentellas, they being so-called after the Italian town where this occurred with monotonous regularity. Indeed, such was the regularity that the unkind might be prompted to suggest that the locals 'hammed it up' for the benefit of the tourists, clerics and doctors who visited Taranto to witness the spectacle.

The last authenticated case of this ergot-induced hysteria was in 1951, in the French town of Pont-Saint-Esprit. Hysteria of a religio-spiritualistic genre was widespread and there were several deaths.

THE THEORY OF EVOLUTION PROPOSED MAN'S DESCENT FROM APES

Darwin never proposed anything of the kind; only his ill-informed detractors chose to believe that he did so that they might ridicule him for it. Darwin simply stated that it was not impossible that man shared a common progenitor with all other mammals, not just monkeys and apes. In any case, Darwin was not the originator of the theories that he postulated, nor did he ever claim to be, openly acknowledging the fact that many others, his own grandfather Erasmus included, had already trod the same path. Darwin himself nominates Aristotle as the father of the theory. Incidentally, the book in which Darwin deals with the origins of man is not *The Origin of the Species*, but *The Descent of Man*.

Darwin's great contribution was a new and more concrete theory on the modification of the species. He named the principle 'natural selection' but later chose to adopt the name that Herbert Spencer gave it – 'survival of the fittest'.

THERE ARE NO STRAIGHT LINES IN NATURE

Many times this 'aphorism' is trotted out – presumably by people who have never seen the perfect symmetry of crystal formation.

THERE IS A 'MISSING LINK' IN THE EVOLUTIONARY CHAIN OF MAN

Evolution is a very long and painful process, and no one of any serious scientific background has ever proposed that there is a yet undiscovered stage in man's development that will prove his descent from apes, because no one, and this includes Darwin, has ever proposed that he did. The notion of a 'missing link', was born out of a total misunderstanding and misrepresentation of Darwin's work.

THICKER GLASSES ARE LESS LIKELY TO CRACK IF FILLED WITH BOILING WATER

Although this seems to be perfectly logical, the exact opposite is the case. When boiling water is poured into a glass the inner surface and adjacent layers are rapidly raised to a high temperature. Glass is an extremely poor conductor of heat, so the expansion of the inner layers causes stress on the non-expanded glass usually culminating in fracture. The ideal receptacle for receiving boiling water is a fine wine glass; laboratory glassware is never thicker than this and is often finer.

When filling a glass to make an Irish coffee, or whatever, some afficionados insist on leaving a teaspoon in the glass, which they maintain will prevent breakage. Obviously, the metal in the spoon will extract some heat from the water, but, if the glass is not up to the task, all the teaspoons in the world will not prevent it breaking.

TIDAL WAVES

These have nothing whatsoever to do with the tide. Actually the term is a total misnomer, the correct name for the phenomenon being 'tsunami'. The solid-wall giants so favoured by the directors of, for example, 'The Poseidon Adventure', simply do not exist in the open sea. Tsunami are caused by violent, usually seismic, disturbances on the sea-bed, which cause a long, low and incredibly fast-moving wave; they can travel at anything up to 500 miles per hour. If one of these ripped under an ocean going liner, it is doubtful whether the captain and crew would even be aware of the fact. They do begin to bank up as they near the shore, just like any other wave, but unlike normal waves, they bank up to their gargantuan proportions due to their phenomenal speeds.

None of this, however, belies the cataclysmic force with which these strike land. The most violent so far recorded was that which struck Ishigaki Island in the Ryukyu Chain that runs between Japan and Formosa. It hit the island on 24 April 1971 and flung a 750-ton block of coral 2½ kilometers inland. The term derives from the Japanese and, loosely translated, means overflowing wave.

THE TITANIC'S BAND'S SWAN SONG
Although the band did play on bravely, they were not playing 'Nearer My God To Thee' – hardly a tune likely to boost the doubtless flagging morale of the passengers! Survivors recall that the ship's band continued to play ragtime until the bridge became submerged and, at that point, they began playing 'Autumn' but never got to the end of the piece. No members of the band survived the tragedy.

TOBACCO AND ITS INTRODUCTION TO ENGLAND BY RALEIGH
The issue as to who was actually responsible is clouded to say the least, but one thing is clear, it was not Raleigh. The two most likely culprits are Sir John Hawkins and Drake. In the records of his 1565 visit to Florida, Hawkins certainly mentions the smoking of tobacco, but does not state whether or not samples were brought back. When Drake returned from the New World in 1586, it does seem fairly certain that he presented Raleigh with pipes and tobacco; the latter being responsible only for the introduction of the habit into court circles.

SWEENY TODD WAS A REAL PERSON
There never was a Sweeny Todd, the mad barber of Fleet Street. He was pure fiction.

MADAME TUSSAUD'S AND THE CHALLENGE TO SPEND ONE NIGHT THERE

This yarn is already well over a century old and still going strong. The myth that there was a challenge and a cash prize for anyone who could stay alone for one night in the Chamber of Horrors first reared its head in 1850 after Dickens, writing in a magazine entitled *All Year Round*, discussed the amount of courage required to undertake a daytime visit, let alone spend a minute in there in the dark. The whole thing got completely out of hand and the museum is still receiving letters from would-be heroes wishing to pick up a gauntlet that has never been cast down. Over the years the myth has been embellished from time to time with tales of unsuccessful challengers being dragged out in the morning blubbering and jibbering, never again to emerge from some lunatic asylum or another.

U

UNDERTOW

One can often find extremely dangerous currents near the shore, but there is no such thing as an 'undertow' that can whisk unwary bathers out to sea. To create a constant flow of sufficient strength to perform such a feat, there would have to be a continual shoreward flow of equal force; a sort of aquatic version of the looped conveyor belt that you see at supermarket checkouts. There is a seaward pull generated by each wave as it falls back from the beach, but this is immediately countered by the next shorebound wave.

UNDILUTED ANTI-FREEZE AFFORDS THE BEST PROTECTION FOR ENGINES

This is a very popular but potentially very expensive misconception. In its pure form, ethylene glycol offers next to no protection at all since at temperatures just below the freezing point of water, it turns into useless slush.

'UP GUARDS AND AT 'EM'

Yet another 'Wellingtonism' born in someone's fruitful imagination, for the Duke denied ever having said such a thing when he replied to John William Crocker, British statesman and author, who had written to him asking for confirmation as to whether or not this command had been given at the Battle of Waterloo when ordering the Guards against the French Imperial Guard.

Actually, there is another quotational myth linked to this engagement. When later offered the opportunity to capitulate, the French Imperial Guard did not send a galloper back with the reply: 'The Guard dies, but never surrenders'. Their real riposte was somewhat more succinct – 'Shit!'

USE OF TELEPHONE IN POLICE STATIONS

Only on televsion can arrested persons insist on being allowed to make the ubiquitous 'phone call to my lawyer'. There is no inviolate right of access to a telephone; if the officers in charge of the investigation consider that the suspect's use of a telephone might impede the course of justice, e.g. tipping off his friends that the game is up, permission can be, and often is, refused.

V

THE 'V' SIGN BEGAN AS A DERISORY GESTURE OF ENGLISH ARCHERS

Various engagements with the French throughout the Hundred Years War have been cited as the origin of this sign so favoured by British road-users. The story goes that the French, understandably miffed at constantly getting the pointed end of the stick from the British bowmen, lost what little sang-froid they had left and, before the start of some battle or other, sent word that not only were they going to give the English the biggest seeing-to of their lives, but that afterwards they were going to cut the relevant two fingers from the archers' right hands to stop them drawing bow ever again. One would be forgiven for thinking that any British archer unfortunate enough to fall into French hands would have experienced more extensive personal impromptu surgery, but there it is. French boasts were to no avail and the British bowmen cut them to smithereens yet again. After the blood-bath, they waved their two fingers at what was left of the French army, to add insult to extensive injury.

It is such a lovely story that it is almost a sacrilege to shoot holes in it, but the sign was known long before any such sport with the French – indeed, long before the introduction of the longbow itself which, incidentally, is drawn with three fingers not two. The sign seems to have had associations with the occult in that it was used to ward off the devil, it being directed towards the ground as a block to his horns. Should one of our ancestors have felt sufficiently ill-disposed to one of his neighbours as to wish the devil upon him, then he would have used the sign in the conventional manner. This, it was believed, would bring black fortune to the life of the recipient.

167

Sexual connotations did not rear their ugly heads until much later when the 'V' melded with another two-fingered sign. This gesture, made with the index and little fingers extended from the clenched fist, was intended to represent the horns of the cuckold and was taken as a pretty hefty insult in those days. Gradually, the now traditional 'V' took over, probably because it was a far more easy gesture to make.

WALLABIES ARE ONLY TO BE FOUND LIVING WILD IN AUSTRALASIA

Most northerners are almost blasé about their wild wallabies, but many is the stranger who has taken the pledge after driving through Derbyshire or Staffordshire at night and seeing a group of wallabies boinking around in the headlights.

Ranking as the only marsupial to be found living wild in the British Isles, the northern colonies of wallabies are thriving once again after the terrible winter of 1963 killed over three-quarters of their number. Exactly what the total wallaby population stands at is difficult to determine due to the desolate nature of their habitat and the creatures' natural shyness, but the recuperating herds could number in the region of sixty, all of whom are the descendants of a pair that escaped from a private menagerie in Leek, in 1939.

ROBERT WALPOLE WAS BRITAIN'S FIRST PRIME MINISTER

Quite impossible since the office of Prime Minister did not even exist until 1937. Baldwin was this country's first PM; those before him bore the title of First Lord of the Treasury. In fact, in Walpole's day the term Prime Minister was a term of abuse, and remained so for quite some time after, only being applied to party leaders who were royal toadies and little more than parliamentary mouthpieces for an unpopular monarch. As stated, the office of Prime Minister was raised in 1937, but the plaque outside Number 10 still states that residence to be that of the First Lord of the Treasury.

GEORGE WASHINGTON AND HIS CHERRY TREE

The alleged incident was in fact the brainchild of one Mason Lock Weems, the man who produced the very first biography of Washington in the year after the President's death – 1800 – entitled *Life of George Washington*. The first edition, which was followed by an impressive sixty-nine others, made no mention of the incident, portraying Washington's early life in something less than a page. In the first revised edition the story emerges along with several new 'facts' about the man, all of them the fabrications of Weems.

Weems was soon discovered to be a 'historian' who liked to beef up history to make it more fun. He even admitted as much when publicly challenged about an incident in his biography of William Penn. Complete with times, dates, names, quotations and anecdotal stories, was talk of a treaty with the Plains Indians which was non-existent outside Weems's mind. As for his flight of fancy about Washington and his father's favourite cherry tree, it is amazing that people believed it as long as they did. How could anyone that honest ever succeed in politics?

WATER DRAINING OUT OF SINKS AND ITS ROTATIONAL DIRECTION

The myth that water draining out of sinks and baths rotates one way in the northern hemisphere, and the opposite way in the southern hemisphere, is so well entrenched that, short of flying people south to conduct an experiment, it is impossible to convince them otherwise. There is a force that influences weather formations and very large bodies of water, but a domestic sinkful has nothing to worry about. It used to be thought that this force, the Coriolis Effect, influenced the erosion patterns of rivers, but eventually this was disproved since even a river is too small a body of water to respond.

The cause of the Coriolis Effect is the earth's rotation. Often referred to as a fictitious force, it can best be explained by the illustration of a missile aimed due north from the Equator. To an observer at the launch site, the path of the missile appears true but, since the earth rotates faster at the Equator than it does at the North Pole, an observer in space sees the missile travel in a curve. Coriolis is also responsible for the formation of anticyclones which, unlike cyclones, are light winds. These do circulate in a clockwise direction in the northern hemisphere and vice versa in the southern.

WATER SHOWS BLUE BECAUSE IT REFLECTS THE SKY

There is no reflective relationship between the sky and any terrestrial body of water.

Both the upper atmosphere and water are totally devoid of colour, but both are full of microscopic particles which scatter light; especially light from the blue end of the spectrum. The light from the red end of the spectrum is not powerful enough to cut through the blockade, so the overall hue is blue.

The characteristic green of the sea is sometimes due to an abundance of plant life and other times to yellow pigments that result from the decomposition of planktonic life. The yellow mixes with the blue light and transmutes the sea to green.

JAMES WATT INVENTED THE STEAM ENGINE

How many children must have sat listening intently as they were taught that Watt first thought of the principles of steam power when, as a lad, he watched the lid of his mother's kettle rattle as the water boiled, and went on to invent the steam engine. Strange then is it not, that steam engines were commonplace before Watt was even a twinkle in his father's eye. It was Thomas Savery who, in 1698, produced a practical engine that worked on steam condensation. Some say that Edward Somerset, Earl of Worcester, created a steam-powered device as early as 1655, but the machine was hardly a workable proposition. Both Newcomen and Crawley had added developments and innovations to Savery's engine before Watt came up with his first contribution to the steam age in 1765 – the separate condenser.

WEBSTER'S DICTIONARY IS A SPECIFIC PUBLICATION

This is surely the only dictionary to be immortalised in song – 'Just like Webster's Dictionary, we're Morocco bound' – as sung in one of the Hope–Crosby 'Road' films. The first problem is that Webster never called his publication anything of the sort; he always referred to it as *An American Dictionary of the English Language*. Secondly, anyone can employ the title *Webster's Dictionary* since it has fallen to the public domain. In other words, there never really has been a publication of that title, although there are plenty of books on the shelf in America that call themselves such.

THE WEIGHT OF MEDIEVAL ARMOUR WAS EXCESSIVE

Our medieval ancestors were not supermen who were able to strut around the battlefield all day, weighed down by suits of armour so heavy that they had to be lifted on to their horses by cranes, as were the French knights in the film version of 'Henry V'. The average suit weighed between 55 and 60 pounds. The heaviest suit ever produced was made in 1570 by the Royal Workshop at Greenwich for the 3rd Earl of Worcester. That suit weighed a little over 81 pounds, which is several pounds lighter than the full marching kit of a Second World War British infantryman. If one stops to consider how rapidly total fatigue would beset a man clad in a couple of hundred pounds of iron as he wielded a heavy broadsword or a mace and chain, it is evident that all the knights would have had to retire from the field after a matter of minutes.

WELLINGTON AND 'PUBLISH AND BE DAMNED'

When a Paris-based publisher named Stockdale made a thinly disguised blackmail attempt in a letter indicating that, for a financial consideration, such references to Wellington as occurred in the romantic memoirs of one Harriette Wilson could be edited out, Wellington did not challenge him to a duel, nor did he dash the immortal 'Publish and be damned' across the letter in red ink and return it. He did throw the threat back in Stockdale's face with these words, but in a separate letter. Stockdale's original letter is kept at Apsley House and has nothing but the original text upon it. (See also THE

WELSH RAREBIT OR RABBIT

Should you ask for Welsh Rabbit, there are still plenty of people about who will point out, quite incorrectly, that it should be 'Rarebit' – indeed, it is often seen printed as such on menus. The fact of the matter is that the dish is properly called Welsh Rabbit, the name having started out as a dig at the poverty-stricken Welsh unable to afford even a rabbit. It is a similar 'joke' to refer to kippers as Glasgow capons.

WESTMINSTER ABBEY IS AN ABBEY

Not since the days of Henry VIII and the Dissolution of the Monasteries has this building been an abbey, if only for the simple reason that there has not been an abbot in residence since then. The official title since 1560 is The Collegiate Church of Saint Peter at Westminster. Elizabeth I replaced the abbot with a dean.

WHALES ARE INCAPABLE OF SWALLOWING A MAN

That Jonah was swallowed by a whale, is not stated anywhere in the Bible, which only mentions 'a great fish'. Nevertheless, the clearing up of this rather minor misconception has given rise to one of more significance – that no whale is even capable of swallowing a human being. The cachalot or sperm whale is eminently capable of swallowing a man, or two at the same time if it feels so disposed. Some pieces of edible fish found inside these creatures have measured in excess of 6 cubic feet, and whole sharks are by no means an uncommon discovery.

173

WHALES SPOUT WATER FROM THEIR BLOW-HOLES UPON SURFACING

Whales are mammals and can no more tolerate their respiratory system being filled with water than can man. Before sounding, a whale fills its gigantic lungs with air and shuts down its air intake to prevent the invasion by water of its respiratory system. They stay down at considerable depths for periods of up to two hours so, by the time they surface again, that inhaled air is extremely warm and moist; as a result, its exhalation produces a steamy effect similar to that of human breath on a cold day. There could well be some sea water caught up in the plume of water vapour, but only that forced to rise by the animal starting to exhale before breaking surface.

WHITE RHINOS ARE WHITE

Oddly enough, they are exactly the same colour as the common or black rhino; the only difference between the two animals is in the shape of the upper lip. The black rhino is a browser and is distinguishable by its pointed upper lip which is ideally suited for nibbling away at thorny bushes. The white rhino is, on the other hand, a grazer and has a broad, rounded upper lip. It is from this physical characteristic that the animal gets its confusing name; it is a corruption of *wijd* – the Afrikaans for wide. Even the black rhino isn't black; both animals are a sort of grey-brown.

WHITE RUSSIANS

Many of the inhabitants of this constituent republic of the Soviet Union were Tsarist supporters during the revolution, but the area's name has no political significance as opposed to 'Red'. 'Byelorussia', as the place used to be known, was named for its traditional costume of white smock, shoes, trousers, and white homespun coat. 'Byely' is the Russian for white.

WILD ANIMALS IN THE SEWERS

In this country there have been tales of wild pigs in the sewers of London, mutant strains of rats that have grown bigger than cats and are completely unaffected by any poisons known to man, and colonies of gigantic pythons, boas and other amphibious snakes which, as babies, were stuffed down lavatories up and down the country when their owners became bored with them. The recent obsession with pollution has brought further embellishment in that the unusual size and resilience of these creatures is often attributed to the illegal dumping of secret and experimental drugs and chemicals by pharmaceutical companies and other contemporary bogies. Quite what it is that these colonies of gargantuan mutants live on is never made clear. Even if a food chain was established, the staple diet of the last link in the chain would be as impossible to live on as it would be unpleasant to contemplate.

In America, where everything has to be larger than life, they do, of course, have even bigger and better denizens of the drains. The dark sewers of New York are apparently infested with giant, junkie, albino alligators who are permanently smashed out of their minds due to all the drugs flushed down the loos during drugs raids. Once again their existence is explained away by blaming them on holidaymakers returning from Florida with baby reptiles which are subsequently dumped down the lavatory. In Florida itself it is, naturally enough, alligators and, believe it or not, sharks, which have supposedly infiltrated the systems via the sea outlets. It could quite put you off going to the bathroom in case of a back-up in the system.

WITCHES WERE BURNT AT THE STAKE IN ENGLAND

Both England and America refrained from passing this singularly barbaric sentence on 'witches', although it was not uncommon in Scotland. Even after the notorious Salem fiasco of 1692, the twenty condemned were all disposed of by hanging, bar one man pressed to death with stones.

For witches, hanging was the execution method employed in this country, but what the unfortunate individuals went through first is best left unsaid. Certain crimes were punishable by being burnt or 'boyled' alive; a woman who killed her husband, for whatever reason, could be burnt at the stake since her crime was considered 'petty treason'.

The reason that the Roman Catholic Church used to prefer burning 'heretics' alive, was that they liked to believe the ideal of *Ecclesia non novit sanguinem* – 'The Church is untainted with blood'. That must rank as one of the most hypocritical niceties of all time.

WOLVES HUNT IN PACKS AND ARE MAN-KILLERS

Stupidity, ignorance, superstition and fear – man's four greatest enemies – have been responsible for the indiscriminate and wholesale slaughter of these grossly misunderstood, misrepresented and maligned creatures. There is not a single authenticated case in the history of any country, of a man, woman or child being killed by wolves. Wolves have a justified fear of man and run shy of him at every occasion.

The wolf is an extremely responsible parent. It usually mates for life and the young, upon attaining maturity, segregate to themselves mate and hunt; so, the concept of enormous, blood-crazed packs roaming the wilds is utter rubbish. Only in times of extreme food shortage can groups of five or six be seen and these are usually family groups reuniting, so that by strength of numbers they can go after larger game than normal.

Man's concept of this creature is indeed a dichotomy for, on the one hand we have the voracious salivating image, and on the other, the persistent recurrence of tales of abandoned children being taken in and reared by wolves.

WOMEN HAVE ONE LESS RIB THAN MEN

Since, by necessity, ribs come in pairs, it is amazing that this biblically instigated piece of nonsense ever got off the ground. The only bone variance of a numerical nature that occurs in the sexes does so in the coccygeal, or tail, vertebrae where women can sometimes have one less section. There is a rare condition known as cervical rib which produces a single extra rib at the base of the neck, but this is very rare indeed and is as likely to occur in either sex.

THE WRIGHT BROTHERS WERE THE FIRST TO ACHIEVE POWERED FLIGHT

On 9 October 1890, Clement Ader took off in his Eole and flew for a distance of about 50 metres at Armainvilliers, in France. On 6 May 1896, Samuel Pierpont Langley flew his unmanned 'Model 5' a distance of three-quarters of a mile along the Potomac river. It was to be some thirteen years after Ader's quick hop that the Wright brothers' plane left the ground at Kittyhawk to fly for a brief twelve seconds. The real 'first' wholly attributable to the Wrights is that of getting a plane off the ground carrying a passenger; this happened on 14 May 1908 when Wilbur took off with his mechanic, Charles Furness.

It was only later that so much was made of the 1903 flight, so that America could wrongly lay claim to the accolade of having been the first to prove the feasibility of powered flight. At the time, the American press was unanimous in its ridicule of the brothers, and only the *Daily Mail* even bothered to mention the event on this side of the Atlantic.

X

'X's ON BEER CONTAINERS ARE AN INDICATION OF STRENGTH
In bygone days, the Customs and Excise men would stamp an 'X' on a beer barrel to signal that the old ten-shilling duty had been paid for one barrel of standard strength ale. It was the brewers themselves who started adding extra 'X's, leaving the publicans and their customers to assume the contents to be of additional strength or quality.

XMAS IS A SLOPPY MODERN SHORTHAND FOR CHRISTMAS
It is neither sloppy nor modern having been in use since the early part of the fifteenth century. In the Greek alphabet the character 'X' represents 'K' and was used to stand for 'Khristos'.

Y

YANKEE AND YANKEE DOODLE
The ever-present myth that the term 'Yankee' arose from the American Indians' inability to say 'English' or 'Anglais', seems to have been extensively popularised by

James Fenimore Cooper, if not wholly invented by him. The word was developed as a tag for the Dutch settlers of the New England states and derives from 'Jan Kees' – the Dutch for Johnny Cheese.

As for 'Yankee Doodle', albeit a tune of most probably American origin, it appeared in print in England in 1778, some sixteen years before it did in America. It was first sung and played by British, not American, troops in the opening days of the War of Independence, and was intended as an insult to the Colonists. As with so many such wartime slurs, the people against whom they are originally directed adopt them as a badge of honour; the Desert Rats and Old Contemptibles being classic examples. The following extract from a letter sent home by a British officer serving in America at the time illuminates the facts: 'After the affair at Bunker's Hill, the Americans gloried in it. "Yankee Doodle" is now their paean. . . After our rapid successes we held the Yankee in contempt, but it is not a little mortifying to hear them playing this tune when their army marched down to our surrender.'

'YE' AND ITS PRONUNCIATION

When reading signs with pretensions to so-called Old English people invariably pronounce the first word as 'Yee', whereas it should be 'the'.

Both Old English and Icelandic used to have a runic symbol 'þ', which equalled 'th' and was called 'thorn', being named, like other runic symbols, from a word of which it was the initial. Printers used to use the letter 'Y' as a substitute, leaving context to indicate meaning to the reader.

'YELLOW PRESS' DERIVED FROM THE YELLOW KID COMIC STRIP

Chronology firmly disputes this popular misconception. True, Richard Outcault's *The Yellow Kid*, printed in yellow, appeared in William Hearst's *New York Journal* in 1895, at the height of a circulation war with Pulitzer's *New York World* during which each paper tried to outdo the other in the gutter press stakes, but the term was well known at least fifty years before. The tag 'Yellow' is first recorded in 1846 as being used to describe cheap fiction and magazines that were 'bound' in gaudy paper covers to attract the eye; yellow being a much favoured colour. It was later in the same year that the term was first applied to the kind of press better known today for its obsession with posturing 'models' and bingo, rather than truth and reality.

YIDDISH

Yiddish is not another term for Hebrew, nor is it a kind of low Pidgin Hebrew for European Jews. Yiddish is a language in its own right; it belongs to the Indo-European family and is therefore completely removed from the Semitic group of languages. It developed in the Middle Ages when Poland invited the Rhineland Jews to move into Poland for the express purpose of forming a trading class between the nobility and the serfs. The Jews retained their Low German language but began to write it with Hebrew characters. The language grew by absorbing from Polish, Russian and, of course, Hebrew. The original term for the tongue was *Judisch Deutsch* – Jewish German, and 'Yiddish' is a corruption of *Judisch*.

Z

THE ZERO WAS AN INFERIOR FIGHTER
During the fall of Singapore and throughout the Pacific theatre of war, the Zero proved the above to be false, time and time again. The myth that the plane was a cheap copy of an American or British design was so prevalent throughout the war, that it most likely cost a good few pilots their lives through their not taking the plane seriously as an adversary, and thus suffering from terminal surprise. The plane was light and under-armoured by European standards, but, of course, the Japanese pilots were not so bothered about dying as were their opponents, and the tremendous manoeuvrability that the dearth of armour plating afforded the Zero, made it quite formidable in aerial combat.

THINGS YOU DIDN'T KNOW YOU DIDN'T KNOW
Graeme Donald

Tuxedo

Son of a Gun

Gazumping

Flushing Toilets and Thomas Crapper

Hobson's Choice

In Hock

There are fascinating stories about the origins of these—and many more—common expressions. This book tells you all you need to know!

GRAFFITI 5
Nigel Rees

From Bondi Beach to Bexley Heath, no wall has been left unsearched to create this brand new collection of the world's best graffiti. The choicest scribblings have been selected and introduced by Nigel Rees, author of the previous four best-selling books in a world-famous series. Special to this volume is a fascinating look at graffiti in the Soviet Union, where banishment to a Siberian labour camp can be a very real dis-incentive to the Russian Kilroy.

'Graffiti is for people who can't write books' comments an anonymous contributor to **Graffiti** 5 – but that does not mean they can't end up in one!

Graffiti 5 – a must for all fans of wit on walls.

EXCUSES, EXCUSES
Gordon Wood & Ernie Daniels

This is a hilarious collection of the outrageous, imaginative, seldom plausible, excuses used by everyone from Prime Ministers to plumbers. It will give inspiration to all officionados of the 'inventive explanation' and to read it will not only make you laugh at the familiarity of the situations, but it might one day help *you* out of a tight spot. Of course, all these excuses are true, unbelievably true.

Also available in Unwin Paperbacks